Cook's Corner

Muffins
and
Other Bakes

igloobooks

Published in 2018
by Igloo Books Ltd
Cottage Farm
Sywell
NN6 0BJ
www.igloobooks.com

Food photography and recipe development:
© StockFood, The Food Media Agency
Cover image: © iStock / Getty Images
Additional imagery: © iStock / Getty Images

STA002 0218
2 4 6 8 10 9 7 5 3 1
ISBN: 978-1-78810-178-3

Cover designed by Nicholas Gage
Interiors designed by Simon Parker
Edited by Jasmin Peppiatt

Printed and manufactured in China

Cook's Corner

Muffins
and other bakes

Contents

Muffins and other bakes

Muffins

Plain muffins

MAKES: 12 | PREP TIME: 10 MINUTES | COOKING TIME: 20-25 MINUTES

INGREDIENTS

1 large egg

120 ml / 4 fl. oz / ½ cup sunflower oil

120 ml / 4 fl. oz / ½ cup milk

375 g / 12 ½ oz / 2 cups self-raising flour, sifted

1 tsp baking powder

200 g / 7 oz / cup caster (superfine) sugar

METHOD

1. Preheat the oven to 180°C (160°C fan) / 350F / gas 4 and oil 12 silicone muffin cases.

2. Beat the egg in a jug with the oil and milk until well mixed. Mix the flour, baking powder and sugar in a bowl. Pour in the egg mixture and stir just enough to combine.

3. Divide the mixture between the cases and bake for 20-25 minutes.

4. Test with a wooden toothpick; if it comes out clean, the muffins are done.

5. Transfer the muffins to a wire rack and leave to cool completely.

Olive mini muffins

MAKES: 24 | PREP TIME: 15 MINUTES | COOKING TIME: 10-15 MINUTES

INGREDIENTS

2 large eggs

120 ml / 4 fl. oz / ½ cup sunflower oil

180 ml / 6 fl. oz / ⅔ cup Greek yogurt

2 tbsp Parmesan, finely grated

225 g / 8 oz / 1 ½ cup plain (all-purpose) flour

2 tsp baking powder

½ tsp bicarbonate of (baking) soda

½ tsp salt

75 g / 2 ½ oz / ½ cup black olives,
stoned and chopped

2 tbsp fresh rosemary, chopped

METHOD

1. Preheat the oven to 180°C (160°C fan) / 350F /
   gas 4 and line a 24-hole mini muffin tin with
   paper cases.

2. Beat the eggs in a jug with the oil, yogurt and
   cheese until well mixed. Mix the flour, raising
   agents, salt, olives and rosemary in a bowl, then
   pour in the egg mixture and stir just
   enough to combine.

3. Divide the mixture between the paper cases,
   then bake in the oven for 10-15 minutes.

4. Test with a wooden toothpick. If it comes out
   clean, the muffins are done. If not, return to
   the oven for another 3-4 minutes and test again.

5. Serve warm.

9

Parmesan muffins

MAKES: 12 | PREP TIME: 15 MINUTES | COOKING TIME: 10-15 MINUTES

INGREDIENTS

2 large eggs

180 ml / 6 fl. oz / ¾ cup Greek yogurt

100 g / 3 ½ oz / 1 cup Parmesan, grated

120 ml / 4 fl. oz / ½ cup sunflower oil

225 g / 8 oz / 1 ½ cup plain (all-purpose) flour

2 tsp baking powder

½ tsp bicarbonate of (baking) soda

½ tsp salt

METHOD

1. Preheat the oven to 180°C (160°C fan) / 350F / gas 4 and line a 12-hole mini muffin tin with paper cases.

2. Beat the egg in a jug with the yogurt, cheese and oil until combined.

3. Mix the flour, baking powder, bicarbonate of soda and salt in a bowl, then pour in the egg mixture and stir just enough to combine, being careful not to over-mix.

4. Divide the mixture between the paper cases, then bake in the oven for 10–15 minutes.

5. Test with a wooden toothpick; if it comes out clean, the muffins are done. If not, return the muffins to the oven for another 5 minutes.

6. Serve warm.

Crab, chilli and lime muffins

MAKES: 12 | PREP TIME: 15 MINUTES | COOKING TIME: 20-25 MINUTES

INGREDIENTS

2 large eggs

120 ml / 4 fl. oz / ½ cup sunflower oil

180 ml / 6 fl. oz / ¾ cup Greek yogurt

2 tbsp Parmesan, finely grated

150 g / 5 ½ oz / ¾ cup fresh crab meat

1 red chilli (chili), finely chopped

1 lime, juiced and zest finely grated

1 tbsp coriander (cilantro) leaves,
finely chopped

225 g / 8 oz / 1 ½ cup plain (all-purpose) flour

2 tsp baking powder

½ tsp bicarbonate of (baking) soda

½ tsp salt

METHOD

1. Preheat the oven to 180°C (160°C fan) / 350F / gas 4 and oil a 12-hole silicone muffin mould.

2. Beat the eggs in a jug with the oil, yogurt, Parmesan, crab, chilli, lime and coriander until well mixed.

3. Mix the flour, raising agents and salt in a bowl, then pour in the egg mixture and stir just enough to combine.

4. Divide the mixture between the moulds, then bake in the oven for 20-25 minutes.

5. Test with a wooden toothpick. If it comes out clean, the muffins are done.

6. Transfer the muffins to a wire rack and allow to cool.

Cheese and bacon muffins

MAKES: 12 | PREP TIME: 15 MINUTES | COOKING TIME: 20 MINUTES

INGREDIENTS

1 tbsp olive oil

100 g / 3 ½ oz / 1 cup bacon lardons

300 g / 10 ½ oz / 2 cups self-raising flour

150 g / 5 ¼ oz / 1 ½ cups Cheddar cheese, grated

1 tsp mustard powder

1 tsp cracked black pepper

250 ml / 9 fl. oz / 1 cup milk

60 g / 2 oz / ¼ cup unsalted butter, melted

2 large free-range eggs, beaten

METHOD

1. Preheat the oven to 180°C (160°C fan) / 350F / gas 4 and line a 12-hole muffin tin with cases.

2. Heat the oil in a frying pan over a medium heat. Fry the bacon lardons until they are starting to crisp around the edges, then remove from the pan and place onto kitchen paper to drain and cool.

3. In a large mixing bowl, combine the bacon, flour, cheese, mustard powder and pepper.

4. In a separate bowl, whisk together the milk, butter and eggs until frothy.

5. Pour the liquid into the dry ingredients and mix just enough to combine. The mixture should be lumpy and of a thick consistency.

6. Spoon the mixture into the prepared cases and bake in the oven for around 20 minutes until golden. Remove and place onto a wire rack to cool.

Cheese muffins

MAKES: 12 | PREP TIME: 15 MINUTES | COOKING TIME: 20 MINUTES

INGREDIENTS

300 g / 10 ½ oz / 2 cups self-raising flour

100 g / 3 ½ oz Cheddar cheese, grated

100 g / 3 ½ oz mozzarella cheese, grated

1 tsp mustard powder

1 tsp cracked black pepper

250 ml / 9 fl. oz / 1 cup milk

60 g / 2 oz / ¼ cup unsalted butter, melted

2 large free-range eggs, beaten

METHOD

1. Preheat the oven to 180°C (160°C fan) / 350F / gas 4 and line a 12-hole muffin tin with cases.

2. In a large mixing bowl, combine the flour, cheeses, mustard powder and pepper.

3. In a separate bowl, whisk together the milk, butter and eggs until frothy.

4. Pour the liquid into the dry ingredients and mix just enough to combine.

5. Spoon the mixture into the prepared cases and bake in the oven for around 20 minutes until golden. Remove and place onto a wire rack to cool.

Pumpkin muffins

MAKES: 12 | PREP TIME: 15 MINUTES | COOKING TIME: 20-25 MINUTES

INGREDIENTS

1 large egg

120 ml / 4 fl. oz / ½ cup sunflower oil

120 ml / 4 fl. oz / ½ cup milk

150 g / 4 ½ oz / 1 cups pumpkin, finely grated

375 g / 12 ½ oz / 2 cups self-raising flour, sifted

1 tsp baking powder

200 g / 7 oz / cup caster (superfine) sugar

TO DECORATE:

4 tbsp cream cheese

2 tbsp icing (confectioner's) sugar

3 tbsp pumpkin seeds

METHOD

1. Preheat the oven to 180°C (160°C fan) / 350F / gas 4 and line a 12-hole muffin tin with paper cases.

2. Beat the egg in a jug with the oil, milk and grated pumpkin until well mixed. Mix the flour, baking powder and sugar in a bowl. Pour in the egg mixture. Stir to combine. Divide the mixture between the cases and bake for 20-25 minutes.

3. Test with a wooden toothpick. If it comes out clean, the muffins are done.

4. Transfer the muffins to a wire rack and leave to cool completely.

5. Whip the cream cheese with the icing sugar and spread it on top of the muffins with a palette knife. Sprinkle over the pumpkin seeds.

Raisin and oat muffins

MAKES: 12 | PREP TIME: 25 MINUTES | COOKING TIME: 20 MINUTES

INGREDIENTS

1 large egg

120 ml / 4 fl. oz / ½ cup sunflower oil

120 ml / 4 fl. oz / ½ cup oat milk

300 g / 10 ½ oz / 2 cups self-raising flour, sifted

75 g / 2 ½ oz / ½ cup jumbo porridge oats

1 tsp baking powder

200 g / 7 oz / ¾ cup caster (superfine) sugar

75 g / 2 ½ oz / ½ cup raisins

METHOD

1. Preheat the oven to 180°C (160°C fan) / 350F / gas 4 and oil a 12-hole silicone muffin tin.

2. Beat the egg in a jug with the oil and milk until well mixed.

3. Mix the flour with two thirds of the oats and the baking powder, sugar and raisins. Pour in the egg mixture and stir just enough to combine.

4. Spoon the mixture into the moulds and sprinkle with the remaining oats, then bake in the oven for 20 minutes. Test with a toothpick; if it comes out clean, the muffins are done. If not, return to the oven for 5 minutes and test again.

5. Turn the muffins out onto a wire rack and leave to cool before serving.

Blackberry muffins

MAKES: 12 | PREP TIME: 15 MINUTES | COOKING TIME: 25 MINUTES

INGREDIENTS

200 g / 7 oz / ¾ cup caster (superfine) sugar

60 g / 2 oz / ¼ cup unsalted butter, melted

2 large free-range eggs, beaten

300 g / 10 ½ oz / 2 cups self-raising flour

250 ml / 9 fl. oz / 1 cup milk

1 lemon, zest

100 g / 3 ½ oz / ⅔ cup blackberries

METHOD

1. Preheat the oven to 180°C (160°C fan) / 350F / gas 4 and line a 12-hole muffin tray with cases.

2. Beat the sugar and butter together in a large mixing bowl until pale and fluffy. Mix in the eggs.

3. Sift the flour into the eggs and butter mixture and mix gradually, adding the milk to form a batter. Mix through the lemon zest and half the blackberries.

4. Spoon into the prepared cases and bake in the oven for 20-25 minutes until golden and a skewer inserted into the centre of a muffins comes out clean.

5. Top the cooled muffins with the remaining berries and dust with icing sugar if desired.

Chocolate and peanut muffins

MAKES: 12 | PREP TIME: 15 MINUTES | COOKING TIME: 30 MINUTES

INGREDIENTS

200 g / 7 oz / ¾ cup caster (superfine) sugar

300 g / 10 ½ oz / 2 cups self-raising flour

50 g / 1 ¾ oz / ¼ cup cocoa powder

250 ml / 9 fl. oz / 1 cup milk

60 g / 2 oz / ¼ cup unsalted butter, melted

2 large free-range eggs, beaten

100 g / 3 ½ oz / ⅔ cup peanut butter

50 g / 1 ¾ oz salted peanuts

METHOD

1. Preheat the oven to 200°C (180°C fan) / 400F / gas 6 and lightly grease a muffin tin.

2. Mix the sugar, flour and cocoa in a large mixing bowl.

3. In a separate bowl, whisk together the milk, butter and eggs until frothy.

4. Make a well in the centre of the dry ingredients, pour in the wet and mix just enough to combine. Fold through the peanut butter and half of the peanuts.

5. Spoon the mixture into the prepared muffin tin and top with the remaining nuts. Bake in the oven for 30 minutes until risen and a skewer inserted into the centre comes out clean. Remove to cool completely.

Coconut and pineapple muffins

MAKES: 12 | PREP TIME: 20 MINUTES | COOKING TIME: 30 MINUTES

INGREDIENTS

200 g / 7 oz / ¾ cup caster (superfine) sugar

300 g / 10 ½ oz / 2 cups self-raising flour

250 ml / 9 fl. oz / 1 cup milk

60 g / 2 oz / ¼ cup unsalted butter, melted

2 large free-range eggs, beaten

1 tsp vanilla extract

200 g / 7 oz / 1 cup pineapple chunks

150 g / 5 ¼ oz / 1 ½ cups desiccated coconut

250 g / 9 oz / 1 ¼ cup low-fat Greek yogurt

150 g / 5 ¼ oz / 1 ½ cups icing (confectioner's) sugar

METHOD

1. Preheat the oven to 200°C (180°C fan) / 400F / gas 6 and lightly grease a muffin tin.

2. Mix the sugar and flour in a large mixing bowl.

3. In a separate bowl, whisk together the milk, butter, eggs and vanilla extract until frothy.

4. Make a well in the centre of the dry ingredients, pour in the wet and mix just enough to combine.

5. Chop the pineapple into small chunks, setting aside 12 larger pieces and reserving any of the liquid. Stir the chopped pineapple and liquid, and half the coconut, into the muffin mix.

6. Spoon the mixture into the prepared muffin tin. Bake in the oven for 30 minutes until risen and a skewer inserted into the centre comes out clean. Remove to cool completely.

7. Mix together the remaining coconut with the yogurt and icing sugar. Spoon onto the cooled muffins before topping with the reserved pineapple chunks.

Chocolate banana muffins

MAKES: 12 | PREP TIME: 15 MINUTES | COOKING TIME: 20 MINUTES

INGREDIENTS

200 g / 7 oz / 1 ⅓ cups plain (all-purpose) flour

50 g / 1 ¾ oz / ¼ cup cocoa powder

125 g / 4 ¼ oz / ½ cup caster (superfine) sugar

1 tsp baking powder

a pinch of salt

1 egg

100 ml / 3 ½ fl. oz / ½ cup milk

250 g / 9 oz bananas, mashed

50 g / 1 ¾ oz chocolate chips

METHOD

1. Preheat the oven to 200°C (180°C fan) / 400F / gas 6 and line a 12-hole muffin tray with cases.

2. Mix together the flour, cocoa powder, sugar, baking powder and salt in a large mixing bowl.

3. Mix together the egg, milk and bananas in a separate bowl, then pour into the dry ingredients and mix until just combined. Fold through the chocolate chips.

4. Spoon the muffin mixture into the cases and bake in the oven for around 20 minutes until risen and a skewer inserted into the centre of a cake comes out clean.

Chocolate orange muffins

MAKES: 12 | PREP TIME: 2 HOURS | COOKING TIME: 20 MINUTES

INGREDIENTS

1 orange

200 g / 7 oz / ¾ cup caster (superfine) sugar

300 g / 10 ½ oz / 2 cups self-raising flour

150 ml / 5 ¼ fl. oz / ⅔ cup of milk

60 g / 2 oz / ¼ cup unsalted butter, melted

2 large free-range eggs, beaten

1 tsp vanilla extract

200 g / 7 oz orange-flavoured dark chocolate

METHOD

1. Thoroughly wash the orange and place into a saucepan and simmering water. Cook for 2 hours until softened.

2. Drain the orange and then set aside to cool. Cut into quarters and remove the pips. Place into a blender and blend to a pulp.

3. Preheat the oven to 200°C (180°C fan) / 400F / gas 6 and lightly grease a muffin tin.

4. Mix the sugar and flour in a large mixing bowl.

5. In a separate bowl, whisk together the milk, butter, eggs and vanilla extract until frothy.

6. Make a well in the centre of the dry ingredients, pour in the wet and mix just enough to combine. Fold through the orange pulp and break up the chocolate and fold through also.

7. Spoon the mixture into the prepared muffin tin. Bake in the oven for 30 minutes until risen and a skewer inserted into the centre comes out clean. Remove to cool completely.

Lemon and apple muffins

MAKES: 12 | PREP TIME: 15 MINUTES | COOKING TIME: 20 MINUTES

INGREDIENTS

200 g / 7 oz / ¾ cup caster (superfine) sugar

300 g / 10 ½ oz / 2 cups self-raising flour

250 ml / 9 fl. oz / 1 cup milk

60 g / 2 oz / ¼ cup unsalted butter, melted

2 large free-range eggs, beaten

1 lemon, juice and zest

50 g / 1 ¾ oz Bramley apple sauce

METHOD

1. Preheat the oven to 200°C (180°C fan) / 400F / gas 6 and line a 12-hole muffin tray with cases.

2. Mix the sugar and flour in a large mixing bowl.

3. Combine the milk, butter, eggs and lemon and whisk until frothy. Pour into the dry ingredients and mix just enough to combine.

4. Spoon into the muffin cases and bake in the oven for 18-20 minutes until risen and a skewer inserted into the centre of a cake comes out clean. Remove from the oven and leave to cool.

5. Cut a small hole in the top of each muffin and add a spoonful of the apple sauce.

Chocolate and vanilla muffins

MAKES: 12 | PREP TIME: 15 MINUTES | COOKING TIME: 18 MINUTES

INGREDIENTS

200 g / 7 oz / ¾ cup caster (superfine) sugar

300 g / 10 ½ oz / 2 cups self-raising flour

50 g / 1 ¾ oz / ¼ cup cocoa powder

250 ml / 9 fl. oz / 1 cup milk

60 g / 2 oz / ¼ cup unsalted butter, melted

2 large free-range eggs, beaten

1 tsp vanilla extract

sugar crystals, to decorate

METHOD

1. Preheat the oven to 200°C (180°C fan) / 400F / gas 6 and line a 12-hole muffin tray with cases.

2. Mix the sugar, flour and cocoa powder in a large mixing bowl.

3. Combine the milk, butter, eggs and vanilla extract. Whisk until frothy. Pour into the dry ingredients and mix together, but not enough to fully combine so that bits of plain are still visible.

4. Spoon the batter into the muffin cases. Bake in the oven for 18 minutes until a skewer inserted into the centre of a cake comes out clean.

5. Remove from the oven and scatter over the sugar crystals, then leave to cool.

31

Lemon and ricotta muffins

MAKES: 12 | PREP TIME: 15 MINUTES | COOKING TIME: 25 MINUTES

INGREDIENTS

250 g / 9 oz / 1 ⅔ cups plain (all-purpose) flour

125 g / 4 ¼ oz / ½ cup caster (superfine) sugar

1 tsp baking powder

a pinch of salt

3 lemons, zest and juice

1 egg

100 ml / 3 ½ fl. oz / ½ cup milk

250 g / 9 oz / 1 ¼ cup ricotta

METHOD

1. Preheat the oven to 200°C (180°C fan) / 400F / gas 6 and line a 12-hole muffin tray with cases.

2. Mix together the flour, sugar, baking powder, salt and lemon zest in a large mixing bowl.

3. Mix together the egg, milk, ricotta and lemon juice in a separate bowl before pouring into the dry ingredients and mixing until just combined.

4. Spoon the muffin mixture into the cases and bake in the oven for around 25 minutes until risen and a skewer inserted into the centre of a cake comes out clean.

Blueberry muffins

MAKES: 12 | PREP TIME: 15 MINUTES | COOKING TIME: 20 MINUTES

INGREDIENTS

300 g / 10 ½ oz / 1 ⅓ cups caster (superfine) sugar

300 g / 10 ½ oz / 2 cups self-raising flour

250 ml / 9 fl. oz / 1 cup milk

60 g / 2 oz / ¼ cup unsalted butter, melted

2 large free-range eggs, beaten

1 tsp vanilla extract

100 g / 3 ½ oz / ⅔ cup blueberries, washed

METHOD

1. Preheat the oven to 200°C (180°C fan) / 400F / gas 6 and line a muffin tin with cases.

2. Mix the sugar and flour in a large mixing bowl.

3. In a separate bowl, whisk together the milk, butter, eggs and vanilla extract until frothy.

4. Make a well in the centre of the dry ingredients, pour in the wet and mix just enough to combine. Fold through the blueberries.

5. Spoon into the cases and bake in the oven for around 20 minutes or until a skewer inserted into the centre comes out clean. Remove to cool.

Strawberry and chocolate muffins

MAKES: 12 | PREP TIME: 15 MINUTES | COOKING TIME: 30 MINUTES

INGREDIENTS

200 g / 7 oz / ¾ cup caster (superfine) sugar

300 g / 10 ½ oz / 2 cups self-raising flour

250 ml / 9 fl. oz / 1 cup milk

60 g / 2 oz / ¼ cup unsalted butter, melted

2 large free-range eggs, beaten

1 tsp vanilla extract

150 g / 5 ¼ oz strawberries, washed and dehulled

50 g / 1 ¾ oz milk chocolate chips

METHOD

1. Preheat the oven to 200°C (180°C fan) / 400F / gas 6 and lightly grease a muffin tin.

2. Mix the sugar and flour in a large mixing bowl.

3. In a separate bowl, whisk together the milk, butter, eggs and vanilla extract until frothy.

4. Make a well in the centre of the dry ingredients, pour in the wet and mix just enough to combine.

5. Chop the strawberries into small chunks, setting 6 aside for later. Stir the strawberries and chocolate chips into the muffin mix.

6. Spoon the mixture into the prepared muffin tin. Bake in the oven for 30 minutes until risen and a skewer inserted into the centre comes out clean. Remove to cool completely.

7. Halve the remaining strawberries and push half into the top of each muffin.

Chocolate and hazelnut muffins

MAKES: 12 | PREP TIME: 15 MINUTES | COOKING TIME: 30 MINUTES

INGREDIENTS

200 g / 7 oz / ¾ cup caster (superfine) sugar

300 g / 10 ½ oz / 2 cups self-raising flour

50 g / 1 ¾ oz / ¼ cup cocoa powder

250 ml / 9 fl. oz / 1 cup milk

60 g / 2 oz / ¼ cup unsalted butter, melted

2 large free-range eggs, beaten

100 g / 3 ½ oz hazelnut spread

100 g / 3 ½ oz dark chocolate chunks

METHOD

1. Preheat the oven to 200°C (180°C fan) / 400F / gas 6 and lightly grease a muffin tin.

2. Mix the sugar, flour and cocoa in a large mixing bowl.

3. In a separate bowl, whisk together the milk, butter and eggs until frothy.

4. Make a well in the centre of the dry ingredients, pour in the wet and mix just enough to combine. Fold through the hazelnut spread and chocolate chunks.

5. Spoon the mixture into the prepared muffin tin. Bake in the oven for 30 minutes until risen and a skewer inserted into the centre comes out clean. Remove to cool completely.

Chocolate and blueberry muffins

MAKES: 12 | PREP TIME: 20 MINUTES | COOKING TIME: 30 MINUTES

INGREDIENTS

200 g / 7 oz / ¾ cup caster (superfine) sugar

300 g / 10 ½ oz / 2 cups self-raising flour

50 g / 1 ¾ oz / ¼ cup cocoa powder

250 ml / 8 ½ fl. oz / 1 cup milk

60 g / 2 oz / ¼ cup unsalted butter, melted

2 large free-range eggs, beaten

100 g / 3 ½ oz / ⅔ cup blueberries, washed

150 g / 5 ¼ oz cream cheese

50 g / 1 ¾ oz / ½ cup icing (confectioner's) sugar

½ tsp vanilla extract

METHOD

1. Preheat the oven to 200°C (180°C fan) / 400F / gas 6 and lightly grease a muffin tin.

2. Mix the sugar, flour and cocoa in a large mixing bowl.

3. In a separate bowl, whisk together the milk, butter and eggs until frothy.

4. Make a well in the centre of the dry ingredients, pour in the wet and mix just enough to combine. Fold through half the blueberries.

5. Spoon the mixture into the prepared muffin tin. Bake in the oven for 30 minutes until risen and a skewer inserted into the centre comes out clean. Remove to cool completely.

6. Whisk together the cream cheese, icing sugar and vanilla extract. Top the cooled muffins with the cream cheese mixture and cover with the remaining blueberries.

Rose petal mini muffins

MAKES: 24 | PREP TIME: 25 MINUTES | COOKING TIME: 20 MINUTES

INGREDIENTS

1 large egg

120 ml / 4 fl. oz / ½ cup sunflower oil

120 ml / 4 fl. oz / ½ cup milk

1 tbsp rose water

375 g / 12 ½ oz / 2 ½ cups self-raising flour, sifted

1 tsp baking powder

200 g / 7 oz / ¾ cup caster (superfine) sugar

55 g / 2 oz / ½ cup ground almonds

2 tbsp crystallised rose petals

icing (confectioner's) sugar, to dust

TO DECORATE:

225 g / 8 oz / 2 ¼ cups icing (confectioner's) sugar

2-4 tsp rose water

crystallised rose petals

METHOD

1. Preheat the oven to 180°C (160°C fan) / 350F / gas 4 and oil a 24-hole silicone mini muffin mould.

2. Beat the egg in a jug with the oil, milk and rose water until well mixed.

3. Mix the flour, baking powder, sugar, ground almonds and rose petals in a bowl, then pour in the egg mixture and stir just enough to combine.

4. Divide the mixture between the moulds. Bake in the oven for 20 minutes. Test with a wooden toothpick. If it comes out clean, the cakes are done.

5. Transfer the cakes to a wire rack and leave to cool before dusting with icing sugar.

6. To decorate, sieve the icing sugar into a bowl and add just enough rose water to make a thick icing.

7. Spoon the icing over the muffins and decorate with crystallised rose petals.

Chocolate muffins

MAKES: 12 | PREP TIME: 25 MINUTES | COOKING TIME: 20-25 MINUTES

INGREDIENTS

1 large egg

120 ml / 4 fl. oz / ½ cup sunflower oil

120 ml / 4 fl. oz / ½ cup milk

200 g / 7 oz / 1⅓ cups self-raising flour, sifted

175 g / 6 oz / 1¼ cups stoneground wholemeal flour

2 tbsp cocoa powder

2 tsp baking powder

200 g / 7 oz / ¾ cup caster (superfine) sugar

150 g / 5 ½ oz dark chocolate (min. 60% cocoa solids), grated

TO DECORATE:
dark chocolate sauce

1 tsp desiccated coconut

METHOD

1. Preheat the oven to 180°C (160°C fan) / 350F / gas 4 and line a 12-hole muffin tin with paper cases.

2. Beat the egg in a jug with the oil and milk until well mixed. Mix the flours, cocoa, baking powder, sugar and chocolate in a bowl. Pour in the egg mixture and stir just enough to combine.

3. Divide the mixture between the paper cases and bake for 20-25 minutes.

4. Test with a wooden toothpick. If it comes out clean, the cakes are done.

5. Transfer the muffins to a wire rack. Leave to cool.

6. Drizzle the dark chocolate sauce over each muffin and sprinkle with the desiccated coconut.

Pecan mini muffins

MAKES: 24 | PREP TIME: 25 MINUTES | COOKING TIME: 15-20 MINUTES

INGREDIENTS

1 large egg

120 ml / 4 fl. oz / ½ cup sunflower oil

120 ml / 4 fl. oz / ½ cup milk

1 tsp vanilla extract

375 g / 12 ½ oz / 2 ½ cups self-raising flour, sifted

1 tsp baking powder

200 g / 7 oz / 1 ¼ cups soft brown sugar

55 g / 2 oz / ½ cup ground almonds

75 g / 2 ½ oz / ⅔ cup pecan nuts, chopped

METHOD

1. Preheat the oven to 180°C (160°C fan) / 350F / gas 4 and oil a 24-hole silicone mini muffin mould.

2. Beat the egg in a jug with the oil, milk and vanilla extract until well mixed.

3. Mix the flour, baking powder, sugar, ground almonds and pecan nuts in a bowl, then pour in the egg mixture and stir just enough to combine.

4. Divide the mixture between the moulds and bake in the oven for 15-20 minutes.

5. Test with a wooden toothpick. If it comes out clean, the muffins are done.

6. Transfer the muffins to a wire rack and leave to cool completely.

Chocolate and almond muffins

MAKES: 12 | PREP TIME: 25 MINUTES | COOKING TIME: 20-25 MINUTES

INGREDIENTS

1 large egg

125 ml / 4 ½ fl. oz / ½ cup almond oil

125 ml / 4 ½ fl. oz / ½ cup milk

1 tsp almond extract

250 g / 9 oz / 1 ⅔ cups self-raising flour, sifted

100 g / 3 ½ oz / 1 cup ground almonds

50 g / 1 ¾ oz / ½ cup unsweetened cocoa powder, sifted

1 tsp baking powder

200 g / 7 oz / ¾ cup caster (superfine) sugar

icing (confectioner's) sugar, for dusting

METHOD

1. Preheat the oven to 180°C (160°C fan) / 350F / gas 4 and line a 12-hole cupcake tin with paper cases.

2. Beat the egg in a jug with the oil, milk and almond extract until well mixed.

3. Mix the flour, ground almonds, cocoa, baking powder and sugar in a bowl, then pour in the egg mixture and stir just enough to combine.

4. Divide the mixture between the cases, then bake in the oven for 20 minutes. Test with a wooden toothpick; if it comes out clean, the muffins are done.

5. If not, return to the oven for 5 minutes and test again.

6. Transfer to a wire rack and leave to cool before serving, dusted with icing sugar.

Fig and honey muffins

MAKES: 12 | PREP TIME: 25 MINUTES | COOKING TIME: 20-25 MINUTES

●●●●●●●●●●●●●●●●●●●●●●●●●●●

INGREDIENTS

1 large egg

120 ml / 4 fl. oz / ½ cup sunflower oil

120 ml / 4 fl. oz / ½ cup milk

100 g / 3 ½ oz / ⅓ cup runny honey

375 g / 12 ½ oz / 2 ½ cups self-raising flour, sifted

1 tsp baking powder

100 g / 3 ½ oz / ½ cup caster (superfine) sugar

5 fresh figs, chopped into small pieces

METHOD

1. Preheat the oven to 180°C (160°C fan) / 350F / gas 4.

2. Line a 12-hole muffin tin with greaseproof paper.

3. In a bowl, beat the egg with the oil, milk and honey until combined.

4. Mix the flour, baking powder, and sugar in a separate bowl.

5. Pour the egg mixture into the flour bowl and stir just enough to combine, then fold in the fig pieces.

6. Divide the mixture between the paper cases and bake for 20 minutes.

7. Test with a wooden toothpick; if it comes out clean, the muffins are done. If not, return the muffins to the oven for another 5 minutes.

8. Transfer the muffins to a wire rack and leave to cool completely.

Blackcurrant muffins

MAKES: 24 | PREP TIME: 20 MINUTES | COOKING TIME: 15-20 MINUTES

INGREDIENTS

1 large egg

120 ml / 4 fl. oz / ½ cup sunflower oil

120 ml / 4 fl. oz / ½ cup milk

375 g / 12 ½ oz / 2 ½ cups self-raising flour, sifted

1 tsp baking powder

200 g / 7 oz / ¾ cup caster (superfine) sugar

200 g / 7 oz / 1 ⅓ cups blackcurrants

METHOD

1. Preheat the oven to 180°C (160°C fan) / 350F / gas 4 and line a 12-hole muffin tin with paper cases.

2. Beat the egg in a jug with the oil and milk until well mixed.

3. Mix the flour, baking powder and sugar in a bowl. Pour in the egg mixture and stir just enough to combine, then fold in the blackcurrants.

4. Divide the mixture between the paper cases and bake for 15–20 minutes.

5. Test with a wooden toothpick; if it comes out clean, the muffins are done.

6. Remove the muffins to a wire rack and leave to cool completely.

Chocolate chip muffins

MAKES: 12 | PREP TIME: 20 MINUTES | COOKING TIME: 20-25 MINUTES

INGREDIENTS

1 large egg

120 ml / 4 fl. oz / ½ cup sunflower oil

120 ml / 4 fl. oz / ½ cup milk

375 g / 12 ½ oz / 2 ½ cups self-raising flour, sifted

1 tsp baking powder

200 g / 7 oz / ¾ cup caster (superfine) sugar

150 g / 5 ½ oz / 1 cup chocolate chips

METHOD

1. Preheat the oven to 180°C (160°C fan) / 350F / gas 4 and line a 12-hole muffin tin with paper cases.

2. Beat the egg in a jug with the oil and milk until well mixed. Mix the flour, baking powder, sugar and chocolate chips in a bowl. Pour in the egg mixture and stir just enough to combine.

3. Divide the mixture between the paper cases and bake for 20-25 minutes.

4. Test with a wooden toothpick. If it comes out clean, the muffins are done.

5. Transfer the muffins to a wire rack and leave to cool completely.

Fig and orange muffins

MAKES: 12 | PREP TIME: 25 MINUTES | COOKING TIME: 20-25 MINUTES

INGREDIENTS

1 large egg

120 ml / 4 fl. oz / ½ cup sunflower oil

120 ml / 4 fl. oz / ½ cup milk

375 g / 12 ½ oz / 2 ½ cups self-raising flour, sifted

1 tsp baking powder

200 g / 7 oz / ¾ cup caster (superfine) sugar

1 orange, zest finely grated

4 fresh figs, chopped

METHOD

1. Preheat the oven to 180°C (160°C fan) / 350F / gas 4 and line a 12-hole muffin tin with greaseproof paper.

2. Beat the egg in a jug with the oil and milk until well mixed. Mix the flour, baking powder, sugar and orange zest in a bowl. Pour in the egg mix and stir just enough to combine, then fold in the figs.

3. Divide the mixture between the paper cases and bake for 20-25 minutes until a wooden toothpick comes out clean.

4. Transfer the muffins to a wire rack and leave to cool completely.

Poppy seed muffins

MAKES: 12 | PREP TIME: 10 MINUTES | COOKING TIME: 20-25 MINUTES

INGREDIENTS

1 large egg

120 ml / 4 fl. oz / ½ cup sunflower oil

120 ml / 4 fl. oz / ½ cup milk

375 g / 12 ½ oz / 2 ½ cups self-raising flour, sifted

1 tsp baking powder

200 g / 7 oz / ¾ cup caster (superfine) sugar

4 tbsp poppy seeds

METHOD

1. Preheat the oven to 180°C (160°C fan) / 350F / gas 4 and oil 12 silicone muffin cases.

2. Beat the egg in a jug with the oil and milk.

3. Mix the flour, baking powder and sugar in a bowl. Pour in the egg mixture and two tablespoons of poppy seeds. Stir to combine but be sure not to over-stir.

4. Divide the mixture between the muffin cases and sprinkle with the remaining two tablespoons of poppy seeds.

5. Transfer to the oven and bake for 20-25 minutes. If a toothpick comes out clean, the muffins are done.

6. Remove to a wire rack and leave to cool completely.

Blackberry mini muffins

MAKES: 24 | PREP TIME: 20 MINUTES | COOKING TIME: 15-20 MINUTES

INGREDIENTS

1 large egg

120 ml / 4 fl. oz / ½ cup sunflower oil

120 ml / 4 fl. oz / ½ cup milk

375 g / 12 ½ oz / 2 ½ cups self-raising flour, sifted

1 tsp baking powder

200 g / 7 oz / ¾ cup caster (superfine) sugar

200 g / 7 oz / 1 ⅓ cups blackberries

METHOD

1. Preheat the oven to 180°C (160°C fan) / 350F / gas 4 and line a 24-hole mini muffin tin with paper cases.

2. Beat the egg in a jug with the oil and milk until well mixed. Mix the flour, baking powder and sugar in a bowl. Pour in the egg mixture and stir just enough to combine then fold in the blackberries.

3. Divide the mixture between the paper cases and bake for 15-20 minutes until a wooden toothpick comes out clean.

4. Transfer the muffins to a wire rack and leave to cool completely.

Ginger muffins

MAKES: 12 | PREP TIME: 15 MINUTES | COOKING TIME: 20-25 MINUTES

INGREDIENTS

1 large egg

120 ml / 4 fl. oz / ½ cup sunflower oil

120 ml / 4 fl. oz / ½ cup milk

4 pieces stem ginger in syrup, chopped

375 g / 12 ½ oz / 2 cups self-raising flour, sifted

1 tsp baking powder

1 tsp ground ginger

200 g / 7 oz / ¾ cup caster (superfine) sugar

METHOD

1. Preheat the oven to 180°C (160°C fan) / 350F / gas 4 and oil a 12-hole silicone oval muffin mould.

2. Beat the egg in a jug with the oil, milk and stem ginger until well mixed. Mix the flour, baking powder, ground ginger and sugar in a bowl. Pour in the egg mixture and stir just enough to combine.

3. Divide the mixture between the moulds and bake for 20-25 minutes.

4. Test with a wooden toothpick; if it comes out clean, the muffins are done.

5. Transfer the muffins to a wire rack and leave to cool completely.

Chocolate and orange mini muffins

MAKES: 24 | PREP TIME: 15 MINUTES | COOKING TIME: 15-20 MINUTES

INGREDIENTS

1 large egg

120 ml / 4 fl. oz / ½ cup sunflower oil

120 ml / 4 fl. oz / ½ cup milk

1 orange, juice and zest

375 g / 12 ½ oz / 2 ½ cups self-raising flour, sifted

1 tsp baking powder

2 tbsp cocoa powder

75 g / 2 ½ oz / ½ cup chocolate chips

75 g / 2 ½ oz / ½ cup candied orange peel, chopped

200 g / 7 oz / ¾ cup caster (superfine) sugar

METHOD

1. Preheat the oven to 180°C (160°C fan) / 350F / gas 4 and line a 24-hole mini muffin tin with paper cases.

2. Beat the egg in a jug with the oil, milk and orange juice and zest until well mixed. Mix the flour, baking powder, cocoa, chocolate chips, candied peel and sugar in a bowl. Pour in the egg mixture and stir just enough to combine.

3. Divide the mixture between the paper cases and bake for 15-20 minutes until a wooden toothpick comes out clean.

4. Transfer the muffins to a wire rack. Leave to cool.

57

Mixed spice muffins

MAKES: 12 | PREP TIME: 15 MINUTES | COOKING TIME: 20-25 MINUTES

INGREDIENTS

1 large egg

120 ml / 4 fl. oz / ½ cup sunflower oil

120 ml / 4 fl. oz / ½ cup milk

375 g / 12 ½ oz / 2 ½ cups self-raising flour, sifted

1 tsp baking powder

2 tsp mixed spice

200 g / 7 oz / ¾ cup caster (superfine) sugar

METHOD

1. Preheat the oven to 180°C (160°C fan) / 350F / gas 4 and line a 12-hole muffin tin with paper cases.

2. Beat the egg in a jug with the oil and milk until well mixed. Mix the flour, baking powder, mixed spice and sugar in a bowl. Pour in the egg mixture and stir just enough to combine.

3. Divide the mixture between the cases and bake for 20-25 minutes.

4. Test with a wooden toothpick. If it comes out clean, the muffins are done.

5. Transfer the muffins to a wire rack and leave to cool completely.

Peanut muffins

MAKES: 12 | PREP TIME: 15 MINUTES | COOKING TIME: 20-25 MINUTES

INGREDIENTS

1 large egg

120 ml / 4 fl. oz / ½ cup sunflower oil

120 ml / 4 fl. oz / ½ cup milk

375 g / 12 ½ oz / 2 ½ cups self-raising flour, sifted

1 tsp baking powder

200 g / 7 oz / ¾ cup caster (superfine) sugar

150 g / 5 ½ oz / 1 cup peanuts

METHOD

1. Preheat the oven to 180°C (160°C fan) / 350F / gas 4 and line a 12-hole muffin tin with paper cases.

2. Beat the egg in a jug with the oil and milk until well mixed.

3. Mix the flour, baking powder, sugar and peanuts in a bowl. Pour in the egg mixture and stir just enough to combine without over-mixing.

4. Divide the mixture between the paper cases and bake for 20-25 minutes.

5. Test with a wooden toothpick. If it comes out clean, the muffins are done.

6. Transfer the muffins to a wire rack and leave to cool completely.

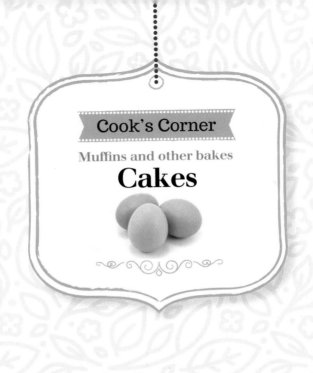

Cook's Corner

Muffins and other bakes

Cakes

Carrot cupcakes

MAKES: 12 | PREP TIME: 20 MINUTES | COOKING TIME: 20 MINUTES

INGREDIENTS

200 g / 7 oz / 1 ¼ cups light brown sugar

200 g / 7 oz / 1 ⅓ cups self-raising flour

1 tsp bicarbonate of (baking) soda

2 tsp mixed spice

2 eggs

150 ml / 5 ¼ fl. oz / ⅔ cup sunflower oil

200 g / 7 oz carrots, grated

100 g / 3 ½ oz / ½ cup unsalted butter, softened

300 g / 10 ½ oz / 1 ¼ cups cream cheese

100 g / 3 ½ oz / 1 cup icing (confectioner's) sugar

1 tsp vanilla extract

1 orange, zested

METHOD

1. Preheat the oven to 180°C (160°C fan) / 350F / gas 4 and line a 12-hole muffin tin with cases.

2. In a large mixing bowl, combine the first four ingredients. In a separate bowl, whisk together the eggs and oil until frothy. Mix into the dry ingredients to form a smooth batter.

3. Fold the grated carrot into the cake mixture before spooning into the cases.

4. Bake in the oven for 20 minutes until a skewer inserted into the centre of a cake comes out clean. Remove to cool on a wire rack.

5. Beat together the butter, cream cheese, icing sugar, vanilla and orange zest. Pipe the icing onto the cooled cakes. Decorate with a sugar carrot if desired.

Mini apricot loaf cakes

SERVES: 12 | PREP TIME: 10 MINUTES | COOKING TIME: 15-20 MINUTES

INGREDIENTS

110 g / 4 oz / ⅔ cup self-raising flour, sifted

110 g / 4 oz / ½ cup caster (superfine) sugar

110 g / 4 oz / ½ cup butter, softened

2 large eggs

1 tsp vanilla extract

75 g / 2 ½ oz / ⅓ cup dried apricots, chopped

METHOD

1. Preheat the oven to 190°C (170°C fan) / 375F / gas 5 and oil a 12-hole silicone mini loaf cake mould.

2. Combine the flour, sugar, butter, eggs and vanilla extract in a bowl and whisk together for 2 minutes or until smooth. Fold in the chopped apricots.

3. Divide the mixture between the moulds, then transfer to the oven and bake for 15-20 minutes.

4. Test with a wooden toothpick. If it comes out clean, the cakes are done.

5. Transfer the cakes to a wire rack and leave to cool completely.

Chocolate ganache gateau

SERVES: 10-12 | PREP TIME: 4 HOURS 30 MINUTES | COOKING TIME: 45 MINUTES

INGREDIENTS

FOR THE CAKE:

110 g / 4 oz / ⅔ cup self-raising flour

28 g / 1 oz / ¼ cup unsweetened cocoa powder

1 tsp baking powder

110 g / 4 oz / ½ cup caster (superfine) sugar

110 g / 4 oz / ½ cup butter

2 large eggs

FOR THE GANACHE:

300 ml / 10 ½ fl. oz / 1 ¼ cups double (heavy) cream

300 g / 10 ½ oz dark chocolate, chopped

75 g / 2 ½ oz / ⅓ cup butter, cubed

FOR THE WHITE CHOCOLATE CURLS:

100 g / 3 ½ oz white chocolate

METHOD

1. Preheat the oven to 180°C (160°C fan) / 350F / gas 4. Grease and line a 20 cm round spring-form cake tin.

2. Whisk together the cake ingredients with an electric whisk. Scrape the mixture into the tin and bake for 30-35 minutes.

3. The cake is ready when a toothpick inserted comes out clean.

4. Transfer the cake to a wire rack to cool before slicing in half horizontally.

5. To make the ganache, bring the cream to simmering point then pour it over the chocolate and stir until smooth.

6. Blend in the butter with a stick blender.

7. Clean the cake tin and line with clingfilm. Put a cake layer in the tin. Pour over half the ganache.

8. Top with the second cake layer and pour the rest of the ganache on top. Level the surface and chill for 4 hours.

9. Melt the white chocolate in a microwave or bain-marie and spread it onto a clean chopping board or marble slab.

10. When it has set, but before it becomes brittle, use a wallpaper scraper to make it into curls. Use these to decorate the cake, then serve.

Cranberry sponges

MAKES: 6 | PREP TIME: 15 MINUTES | COOKING TIME: 20-25 MINUTES

INGREDIENTS

175 g / 6 oz / 1 ¼ cups self-raising flour

2 tsp baking powder

175 g / 6 oz / ¾ cup caster (superfine) sugar

175 g / 6 oz / ¾ cup butter

3 large eggs

200 g / 7 oz / 1 ⅓ cups cranberries

METHOD

1. Preheat the oven to 180°C (160°C fan) / 350F / gas 4 and grease and 6 individual cake tins.

2. Put the flour, baking powder, sugar, butter and eggs in a mixing bowl and whisk them together with an electric whisk for 4 minutes or until pale and well whipped.

3. Fold in the cranberries and divide the mixture between the tins.

4. Bake for 20-25 minutes. The cakes are ready when a toothpick inserted comes out clean.

5. Transfer the cakes to a wire rack to cool completely.

Almond and honey cake

SERVES: 8 | PREP TIME: 25 MINUTES | COOKING TIME: 40 MINUTES

INGREDIENTS

55 g / 2 oz / ⅓ cup self-raising flour, sifted

55 g / 2 oz / ½ cup ground almonds

55 g / 2 oz / ½ cup caster (superfine) sugar

110 g / 4 oz / ⅓ cup honey

110 g / 4 oz / ½ cup butter, softened

2 large eggs

1 tsp almond essence

FOR THE TOPPING:

4 tbsp runny honey

60 g / 2 oz flaked (slivered) almonds

METHOD

1. Preheat the oven to 190°C (170°C fan) / 375F / gas 5 and grease and line a 23 cm round cake tin.

2. Combine the flour, ground almonds, sugar, honey, butter, eggs and almond essence in a bowl and whisk together for 2 minutes.

3. Scrape the mixture into the prepared tin. Bake for 35 minutes. Test with a wooden toothpick. If it comes out clean, the cake is done.

4. To make the topping, mix the honey and almonds together and spoon it on top of the cake. Return the cake to the oven for 5 minutes or until the honey melts into the cake and the almonds turn golden.

5. Transfer the cake to a wire rack to cool.

Pink icing cupcakes

MAKES: 12 | PREP TIME: 15 MINUTES | COOKING TIME: 10-15 MINUTES

INGREDIENTS

110 g / 4 oz / ½ cup butter, softened

110 g / 4 oz / ½ cup caster (superfine) sugar

2 large eggs

110 g / 4 oz / ⅔ cup self-raising flour, sifted

1 tsp vanilla extract

FOR THE TOPPING:

110 g / 4 oz / ½ cup butter, softened

225 g / 8 oz / 2 ¼ cups icing (confectioner's) sugar

2 tbsp milk

3-4 drops of pink food dye

edible pink sprinkles or sugar pearls, to decorate

METHOD

1. Preheat the oven to 190°C (170°C fan) / 375F / gas 5 and line a 12-hole cupcake tin with paper cases.

2. Combine the butter and sugar in a large mixing bowl. Add the eggs and mix until light and fluffy.

3. Add the flour and vanilla extract to the mixture, stirring continuously until well combined.

4. Divide the mixture between the paper cases, then bake for 15–20 minutes.

5. Test with a wooden toothpick; if it comes out clean, the cakes are done.

6. Transfer the cakes to a wire rack and leave to cool.

7. Meanwhile, to make the buttercream, beat the butter with a wooden spoon until fluffy and then gradually beat in the icing sugar. Whisk in the milk and pink food dye until the buttercream is smooth.

8. Pipe or spread the buttercream onto the cakes once they have fully cooled.

9. Sprinkle each cupcake with some edible pink sprinkles or sugar pearls.

Almond cakes

MAKES: 6 | PREP TIME: 10 MINUTES | COOKING TIME: 20-25 MINUTES

INGREDIENTS

55 g / 2 oz / ⅓ cup self-raising flour, sifted

1 tsp baking powder

55 g / 2 oz / ½ cup ground almonds

110 g / 4 oz / ½ cup caster (superfine) sugar

110 g / 4 oz / ½ cup butter, softened

2 large eggs

METHOD

1. Preheat the oven to 190°C (170°C fan) / 375F / gas 5 and oil a 6-hole silicone tartlet mould or 6 individual tartlet tins.

2. Combine all of the ingredients in a bowl and whisk together for 2 minutes or until smooth.

3. Divide between the tins and bake for 20-25 minutes.

4. Test with a wooden toothpick. If it comes out clean, the cakes are done.

5. Transfer the cakes to a wire rack to cool before serving.

Chocolate and almond marble loaf

SERVES: 8 | PREP TIME: 15 MINUTES | COOKING TIME: 45 MINUTES

INGREDIENTS

100 g / 3 ½ oz / ⅔ cup self-raising flour

1 tsp baking powder

50 g / 1 ¾ oz / ½ cup ground almonds

150 g / 5 ½ oz / ⅔ cup caster (superfine) sugar

150 g / 5 ½ oz / ⅔ cup butter

3 large eggs

2 tbsp cocoa powder

4 tbsp flaked (slivered) almonds

METHOD

1. Preheat the oven to 180°C (160°C fan) / 350F / gas 4 and line a loaf tin with greaseproof paper.

2. Sieve the flour and baking powder into a mixing bowl then add the ground almonds, sugar, butter and eggs. Whisk with an electric whisk for 4 minutes. Divide the mixture into 2 bowls. Mix the cocoa powder with 2 tablespoons of hot water. Stir it into one of the bowls.

3. Spoon the mixture into the tin, alternating between chocolate and plain, then draw a knife down the centre to marble.

4. Sprinkle with flaked almonds and bake for 45 minutes. The cake is ready when a toothpick inserted in the centre comes out clean.

5. Transfer the cake to a wire rack to cool.

Gluten-free coconut cake

SERVES: 8-10 | PREP TIME: 10 MINUTES | COOKING TIME: 50 MINUTES

INGREDIENTS

225 g / 8 oz / 1 cup butter, softened

225 g / 8 oz / 1 cup caster (superfine) sugar

4 large eggs, beaten

225 g / 4 ½ oz / 1 ½ cups rice flour

1 tsp baking powder

100 g / 3 ½ oz / 1 cup desiccated coconut

METHOD

1. Preheat the oven to 180°C (160°C fan) / 350F / gas 4.

2. Grease and line a 23 cm round cake tin with greaseproof paper

3. Cream the butter and sugar together until combined then add the eggs and whisk until light and fluffy.

4. Fold in the flour, baking powder and coconut, then scrape the mixture into the tin.

5. Bake the cake for 50 minutes or until a skewer inserted in the centre comes out clean. If not, return the cake to the oven for another 5 minutes.

Apple and cinnamon cake

SERVES: 8 | PREP TIME: 10 MINUTES | COOKING TIME: 55 MINUTES

INGREDIENTS

300 g / 10 ½ oz / 2 cups self-raising flour

2 tsp ground cinnamon

2 tsp baking powder

250 g / 9 oz / 1 ½ cups light brown sugar

250 g / 9 oz / 1 ¼ cups butter, softened

5 large eggs

2 eating apples, cored and chopped

METHOD

1. Preheat the oven to 170°C (150°C fan) / 340F / gas 3 and line a large loaf tin with non-stick baking paper.

2. Sieve the flour, cinnamon and baking powder into a mixing bowl and add the sugar, butter and eggs.

3. Beat the mixture with an electric whisk for 4 minutes or until smooth and well whipped. Fold in the chopped apples and scrape the mixture into the loaf tin.

4. Bake for 55 minutes or until a skewer inserted comes out clean.

5. Transfer the cake to a wire rack and leave to cool completely.

73

Honey, walnut and orange cake

SERVES: 8-10 | PREP TIME: 10 MINUTES | COOKING TIME: 35-40 MINUTES

INGREDIENTS

300 g / 10 ½ oz / 2 cups self-raising flour

2 tsp baking powder

125 g / 4 ½ oz / ½ cup caster (superfine) sugar

125 g / 4 ½ oz / ⅓ cup runny honey

3 oranges, zested

250 g / 9 oz / 1 ¼ cup butter, softened

5 large eggs

300 g / 10 ½ oz / 2 cups icing (confectioner's) sugar

3 tbsp warm water

50 g / 1 ¼ oz walnuts, chopped

METHOD

1. Preheat the oven to 170°C (150°C fan) / 340F / gas 3.

2. Line a 23 cm round spring form cake tin with greaseproof paper.

3. Sieve the flour and baking powder into a mixing bowl and add the sugar, honey, orange zest, butter and eggs.

4. Beat the mixture with an electric whisk for 3 minutes or until fully combined.

5. Pour the mixture into the cake tin and bake for 35-40 minutes or until a skewer inserted in the centre comes out clean.

6. Transfer the cake to a wire rack and leave to cool completely.

7. Meanwhile, make the icing by combining the icing sugar with a few splashes of warm water (approximately 3 tbsp) until it forms a slightly runny icing.

8. Once the cake has cooled, place it on a large plate and drizzle the icing over the top.

9. Before the icing sets, sprinkle the chopped walnuts on top.

Coconut cake with redcurrant compote

SERVES: 8-10 | PREP TIME: 15 MINUTES | COOKING TIME: 45-55 MINUTES

INGREDIENTS

225 g / 8 oz / 1 cup butter, softened

225 g / 8 oz / 1 cup caster (superfine) sugar

4 large eggs, beaten

225 g / 4 ½ oz / 1 ½ cups self-raising flour

100 g / 3 ½ oz / 1 cup desiccated coconut

FOR THE COMPOTE

100 g / 3 ½ oz / ⅔ cup redcurrants

4 tbsp caster (superfine) sugar

METHOD

1. Preheat the oven to 180°C (160°C fan) / 350F / gas 4 and grease and line a 23 cm round cake tin with greaseproof paper.

2. Cream the butter and sugar together then gradually whisk in the eggs, beating well after each addition.

3. Fold in the flour and coconut then scrape the mixture into the tin.

4. Bake the cake for 45 minutes or until a skewer inserted in the centre comes out clean.

5. Meanwhile, put the redcurrants in a small saucepan with the sugar and a splash of water. Cover and cook for 5 minutes then remove the lid, stir and cook for a few more minutes until the redcurrants start to burst and the juices thicken.

6. Leave the cake to cool for 20 minutes before serving warm with the compote spooned over the top.

Peach cake

SERVES: 12 | PREP TIME: 20 MINUTES | COOKING TIME: 25-30 MINUTES

INGREDIENTS

110 g / 4 oz / ⅔ cup self-raising flour, sifted

110 g / 4 oz / ½ cup caster (superfine) sugar

110 g / 4 oz / ½ cup butter, softened

2 large eggs

300 ml / 10 ½ fl. oz / 1 ¼ cups double (heavy) cream

1 can of peach slices, drained, syrup reserved

1 strawberry, thinly sliced

METHOD

1. Preheat the oven to 190°C (170°C fan) / 375F / gas 5.

2. Line a 23 cm round spring form cake tin with greaseproof paper.

3. Combine the flour, sugar, butter and eggs in a bowl and whisk together for 2-3 minutes until smooth and fully combined.

4. Pour the mixture into the cake tin and bake for 25-30 minutes.

5. Test with a wooden toothpick; if it comes out clean, the cake is done. If not, return the cake to the oven for another 5 minutes.

6. Once cooked, transfer the cake to a wire rack and leave to cool completely.

7. While waiting for the cake to cool, whip the cream until thick. Then, once cooled, cut the cake in half.

8. Separate the two halves and spread the bottom half with a thick layer of the whipped cream, leaving approximately 1cm around the edge of the cream to allow for it to spread out slightly. Then sit the other half of the cake back on top of the cream.

9. Decorate the top of the cake by sitting the peach slices in a symmetrical pattern and then place the slices of strawberry in the centre.

10. Finally, before serving, pour the reserved syrup in between the peach slices to allow it to soak into the cake.

Mini berry cupcakes

MAKES: 36 | PREP TIME: 10 MINUTES | COOKING TIME: 10-15 MINUTES

INGREDIENTS

110 g / 4 oz / 1 cup self-raising flour, sifted

110 g / 4 oz / 1 cup caster (superfine) sugar

110 g / 4 oz / ½ cup butter, softened

2 large eggs

1 tsp vanilla extract

18 raspberries

18 blackberries

METHOD

1. Preheat the oven to 190°C (170°C fan) / 375F / gas 5. Line three 12-hole cupcake tins with paper cases.

2. Combine the flour, sugar, butter, eggs and vanilla extract in a bowl and whisk together for 2 minutes or until smooth.

3. Divide the mixture between the paper cases and press a berry into the top of each one.

4. Transfer the tins to the oven and bake for 10-15 minutes.

5. Test with a wooden toothpick. If it comes out clean, the cakes are done.

6. Transfer the cakes to a wire rack and leave to cool completely.

Chocolate mandarin cake

SERVES: 8 | PREP TIME: 10 MINUTES | COOKING TIME: 35 MINUTES

INGREDIENTS

300 g / 10 ½ oz / 2 cups self-raising flour

28 g / 1 oz / ¼ cup unsweetened cocoa powder

2 tsp baking powder

250 g / 9 oz / 1 ¼ cup caster (superfine) sugar

250 g / 9 oz / 1 ¼ cup butter, softened

5 large eggs

1 can mandarin segments in syrup, drained

METHOD

1. Preheat the oven to 170°C (150°C fan) / 340F / gas 3 and butter a 23 cm round cake tin.

2. Sieve the flour, cocoa and baking powder into a mixing bowl and add sugar, butter and eggs.

3. Beat the mixture with an electric whisk for 4 minutes until smooth.

4. Arrange the mandarin segments in the bottom of the tin and spoon the cake mixture on top.

5. Bake for 35 minutes or until a skewer inserted comes out clean.

6. Leave the cake to cool for 20 minutes before turning out onto a serving plate.

Apple and poppy seed cake

SERVES: 8 | PREP TIME: 10 MINUTES | COOKING TIME: 45 MINUTES

INGREDIENTS

300 g / 10 ½ oz / 2 cups self-raising flour

2 tsp baking powder

250 g / 9 oz / 1 ½ cups dark brown sugar

250 g / 9 oz / 1 ¼ cups butter, softened

5 large eggs

2 tbsp poppy seeds

1 tbsp caster (superfine) sugar

3 eating apples, cored and sliced

METHOD

1. Preheat the oven to 170°C (150°C fan) / 340F / gas 3 and butter a round baking dish.

2. Sieve the flour and baking powder into a mixing bowl and add the brown sugar, butter, eggs and half the poppy seeds.

3. Beat the mixture with an electric whisk for 4 minutes or until smooth.

4. Sprinkle the rest of the poppy seeds and the caster sugar over the base of the baking dish and arrange the apple slices on top.

5. Spoon the cake mixture on top of the apple and bake for 45 minutes or until a skewer inserted comes out clean.

6. Leave the cake to cool for 20 minutes before turning out onto a serving plate.

Banana and walnut loaf cake

SERVES: 8 | PREP TIME: 10 MINUTES | COOKING TIME: 55 MINUTES

INGREDIENTS

3 very ripe bananas

110 g / 4 oz / ½ cup soft light brown sugar

2 large eggs

120 ml / 4 fl. oz / ½ cup sunflower oil

225 g / 8 oz / 1 ½ cup plain (all-purpose) flour

1 tsp bicarbonate of (baking) soda

75 g / 2 ½ oz / ⅔ cup walnuts, chopped

METHOD

1. Preheat the oven to 170°C (150°C fan) / 340F / gas 3 and line a long thin loaf tin with non-stick baking paper.

2. Mash the bananas roughly with a fork then whisk in the sugar, eggs and oil.

3. Sieve the flour and bicarbonate of soda into the bowl. Add the chopped walnuts. Stir just enough to evenly mix all the ingredients together.

4. Scrape the mixture into the loaf tin and bake for 55 minutes or until a skewer inserted comes out clean.

5. Transfer the cake to a wire rack and leave to cool completely.

Poppy seed cake

SERVES: 8 | PREP TIME: 15 MINUTES | COOKING TIME: 55 MINUTES

INGREDIENTS

225 g / 8 oz / 1 ½ cups self-raising flour

100 g / 3 ½ oz / ½ cup butter, cubed

100 g / 3 ½ oz / ½ cup caster (superfine) sugar

2 tbsp poppy seeds

1 large egg

75 ml / 3 ½ fl. oz / ⅓ cup whole milk

icing (confectioner's) sugar, to decorate

METHOD

1. Preheat the oven to 180°C (160°C fan) / 350F / gas 4 and line a 23 cm round cake tin with non-stick baking paper.

2. Sieve the flour into a mixing bowl and rub in the butter until it resembles fine breadcrumbs then stir in the sugar and poppy seeds.

3. Lightly beat the egg with the milk and stir it into the dry ingredients until just combined.

4. Scrape the mixture into the tin. Bake for 55 minutes or until a skewer inserted comes out clean. Transfer the cake to a wire rack and leave to cool completely.

5. Sprinkle with icing sugar to serve.

Light fruit cake

SERVES: 8 | PREP TIME: 15 MINUTES | COOKING TIME: 55 MINUTES

INGREDIENTS

225 g / 8 oz / 1 ½ cups self-raising flour

100 g / 3 ½ oz / ½ cup butter, cubed

100 g / 3 ½ oz / ½ cup caster (superfine) sugar

100 g / 3 ½ oz / ⅔ cup mixed dried fruit

8 glacé cherries, quartered

1 tsp grated lemon zest

1 large egg

75 ml / 2 ½ fl. oz / 1 ⅓ cups whole milk

METHOD

1. Preheat the oven to 180°C (160°C fan) / 350F / gas 4 and line a loaf tin with non-stick baking paper.

2. Sieve the flour into a mixing bowl and rub in the butter until it resembles fine breadcrumbs, then stir in the sugar, dried fruit, cherries and lemon zest.

3. Lightly beat the egg with the milk and stir it into the dry ingredients until just combined.

4. Scrape the mixture into the loaf tin and bake for 55 minutes or until a skewer inserted comes out clean. Transfer the cake to a wire rack and leave to cool completely.

Vanilla bundt cake

MAKES: 12 | **PREP TIME:** 30 MINUTES | **COOKING TIME:** 15-20 MINUTES

INGREDIENTS

110 g / 4 oz / ½ cup butter

55 g / 2 oz / ⅓ cup plain (all-purpose) flour

55 g / 2 oz / ½ cup ground almonds

110 g / 4 oz / 1 cup icing (confectioner's) sugar, plus extra to sprinkle on top

3 large egg whites

1 vanilla pod, seeds only

METHOD

1. Preheat the oven to 170°C (150°C fan) / 340F / gas 3 and oil and flour a 26 cm bundt tin.

2. In a small pan, heat the butter until it foams and starts to smell nutty, then leave to cool.

3. Combine the flour, ground almonds and icing sugar in a bowl and whisk in the egg whites and vanilla seeds.

4. Pour the cooled butter through a sieve into the bowl and whisk into the mixture until evenly mixed.

5. Spoon the mixture carefully into the bundt tin then transfer the tin to the oven and bake for 15-20 minutes.

6. Test with a wooden toothpick; if it comes out clean, the cake is done. If not, return the cake to the oven for another 5 minutes.

7. Once cooked, remove the cake from the oven and leave to cool in its tin for at least 20 minutes. Then, carefully remove from the tin, place flat side down on a wire rack and leave to cool further.

8. When ready to serve, sprinkle the cake with icing sugar.

Pineapple upside-down cake

SERVES: 8 | PREP TIME: 15 MINUTES | COOKING TIME: 35 MINUTES

INGREDIENTS

300 g / 10 ½ oz / 2 cups self-raising flour

2 tsp baking powder

250 g / 9 oz / 1 ¼ cups caster (superfine) sugar

250 g / 9 oz / 1 ¼ cups butter, softened

5 large eggs

4 tbsp raspberry jam (jelly)

4 canned pineapple rings, drained

METHOD

1. Preheat the oven to 170°C (150°C fan) / 340F / gas 3 and butter a 23 cm round cake tin.

2. Sieve the flour and baking powder into a mixing bowl and add sugar, butter and eggs.

3. Beat the mixture with an electric whisk for 4 minutes or until smooth.

4. Spread the jam over the base of the cake tin and arrange the pineapple rings on top.

5. Spoon in the cake mixture and bake for 35 minutes or until a skewer inserted comes out clean.

6. Leave the cake to cool for 20 minutes before turning out onto a serving plate.

Chocolate truffle loaf cake

SERVES: 8-10 | PREP TIME: 15 MINUTES | COOKING TIME: 40-50 MINUTES

INGREDIENTS

600 g / 1 lb 5 oz / 2 ¾ cups cream cheese

150 ml / 5 fl. oz / ⅔ cup soured cream

175g / 6 oz / ¾ cup caster (superfine) sugar

2 large eggs

1 egg yolk

2 tbsp plain (all-purpose) flour

2 tbsp cocoa powder, plus extra for dusting

200 g / 7 oz dark chocolate (min. 60% cocoa solids), melted

METHOD

1. Preheat the oven to 180°C (160°C fan) / 350F / gas 4 and grease and line a large loaf tin with greaseproof paper.

2. Put all of the ingredients in a bowl and whisk together until smooth. Scrape the mixture into the loaf tin and level the top with a palette knife.

3. Put the loaf tin in a large roasting tin and pour around enough boiling water to come half way up the side of the loaf tin.

4. Bake the cake for 40-50 minutes or until the centre is only just set.

5. Leave to cool completely in the tin then refrigerate for 2 hours before turning out and dusting with cocoa.

Gluten- and dairy-free banana loaf cake

SERVES: 8 | PREP TIME: 10 MINUTES | COOKING TIME: 55 MINUTES

INGREDIENTS

3 very ripe bananas

110 g / 4 oz / ½ cup caster (superfine) sugar

2 large eggs

120 ml / 4 fl. oz / ½ cup sunflower oil

175 g / 6 oz / 1 ¼ cups rice flour

2 tsp baking powder

50 g / 1 ¾ oz / ⅓ cup ground almonds

METHOD

1. Preheat the oven to 170°C (150°C fan) / 340F / gas 3 and line a medium loaf tin with non-stick baking paper.

2. Mash the bananas well with a fork then whisk in the sugar, eggs and oil.

3. Sieve the rice flour and baking powder into the bowl. Add the ground almonds. Stir to evenly mix all the ingredients together.

4. Scrape the mixture into the loaf tin and bake for 55 minutes or until a skewer inserted comes out clean.

5. Transfer the cake to a wire rack and leave to cool completely.

Peach cake with lemon thyme sugar

SERVES: 8 | PREP TIME: 25 MINUTES | COOKING TIME: 55 MINUTES

INGREDIENTS

225 g / 8 oz / 1 ½ cups self-raising flour

100 g / 3 ½ oz / ½ cup butter, cubed

100 g / 3 ½ oz / ½ cup caster (superfine) sugar

1 large egg

75 ml / 2 ½ fl. oz / ⅓ cup whole milk

4 peaches, halved and stoned

FOR THE LEMON THYME SUGAR:

1 tbsp lemon thyme leaves

60 g / 2 oz / ¼ cup caster (superfine) sugar

TO DECORATE:

150 g / 5 ¼ oz / 1 ¼ cups cream cheese

50 g / 1 ¾ oz / ½ cup icing (confectioner's) sugar

METHOD

1. Preheat the oven to 180°C (160°C fan) / 350F / gas 4 and butter a round baking dish.

2. Firstly, make the lemon thyme sugar. Bruise the thyme leaves with a pestle and mortar then add half the sugar and pound again. Stir in the rest of the sugar and set aside.

3. Sieve the flour into a mixing bowl and rub in the butter until it resembles fine breadcrumbs, then stir in the sugar.

4. Lightly beat the egg with the milk and stir it into the dry ingredients until just combined.

5. Scrape the mixture into the baking dish and level the surface then press in the peach halves, cut side up.

6. Bake the cake for 55 minutes or until a skewer inserted comes out clean.

7. Transfer the cake to a wire rack and leave to cool completely.

8. Whisk together the lemon thyme sugar, cream cheese and icing sugar. Top the cooled cake with the cream cheese mixture and spread evenly.

Clementine upside-down cake

SERVES: 8 | PREP TIME: 15 MINUTES | COOKING TIME: 35 MINUTES

INGREDIENTS

300 g / 10 ½ oz / 2 cups self-raising flour

2 tsp baking powder

250 g / 9 oz / 1 ¼ cups caster (superfine) sugar

250 g / 9 oz / 1 ¼ cups butter, softened

5 large eggs

4 tbsp golden syrup

4 clementines, thinly sliced

METHOD

1. Preheat the oven to 170°C (150°C fan) / 340F / gas 3 and butter a 23 cm round cake tin.

2. Sieve the flour and baking powder into a bowl and add the sugar, butter and eggs.

3. Beat the mixture with an electric whisk for 4 minutes or until smooth and well whipped.

4. Spread the golden syrup over the base of the cake tin and arrange the clementine slices on top and up the sides of the tin.

5. Spoon in the cake mixture and bake for 35 minutes or until a skewer inserted in the centre comes out clean.

6. Leave the cake to cool for 20 minutes before turning out onto a serving plate.

Strawberry meringues

SERVES: 6 | PREP TIME: 10 MINUTES | COOKING TIME: 30-35 MINUTES

INGREDIENTS

110 g / 4 oz / ⅔ cup self-raising flour, sifted

1 tsp baking powder

110 g / 4 oz / ½ cup caster (superfine) sugar

110 g / 4 oz / ½ cup butter, softened

2 large eggs

6 tbsp strawberry jam (jelly)

400 g / 14 oz strawberries, sliced

2 tbsp toasted flaked (slivered) almonds

2 tbsp pistachio nuts, chopped

FOR THE MERINGUE:

4 large egg whites

110 g / 4 oz / ½ cup caster (superfine) sugar

METHOD

1. Preheat the oven to 190°C (170°C fan) / 375F / gas 5. Oil a 6-hole silicone tartlet mould or 6 tartlet tins.

2. Combine the flour, baking powder, sugar, butter and eggs in a bowl. Whisk together for 2 minutes.

3. Divide between the tins and bake for 20-25 minutes. Test with a wooden toothpick. If it comes out clean, the cakes are done. Turn the cakes out onto a baking tray. Spread the tops with the jam.

4. Whisk the egg whites until stiff, then whisk in half the sugar until the mixture is shiny.

5. Fold in the remaining sugar then spoon the meringue on top of the cakes, allowing it to ooze down the sides.

6. Return the cakes to the oven and cook for 10 minutes. Leave the cakes to cool before topping them with sliced strawberries and nuts.

Chocolate almond cake

SERVES: 8 | PREP TIME: 10 MINUTES | COOKING TIME: 45-50 MINUTES

INGREDIENTS

100 g / 3 ½ oz / ⅔ cup self-raising flour

1 tsp baking powder

2 tbsp cocoa powder

50 g / 1 ¾ oz / ½ cup ground almonds

150 g / 5 ½ oz / ⅔ cup caster (superfine) sugar

150 g / 5 ½ oz / ⅔ cup butter

3 large eggs

100 g / 3 ½ oz dark chocolate (min. 60% cocoa solids), chopped

100 g / 3 ½ oz / ⅔ cup blanched almonds

METHOD

1. Preheat the oven to 180°C (160°C fan) / 350F / gas 4 and butter a terrine dish.

2. Sieve the flour, baking powder and cocoa into a mixing bowl then add the ground almonds, sugar, butter and eggs and whisk with an electric whisk for 4 minutes.

3. Fold in the chocolate and almonds. Spoon into the terrine, then bake for 45-50 minutes.

4. The cake is ready when a toothpick inserted in the centre comes out clean.

5. Transfer the cake to a wire rack to cool completely.

Plum and honey loaf cake

SERVES: 8 | PREP TIME: 15 MINUTES | COOKING TIME: 55 MINUTES

INGREDIENTS

225 g / 8 oz / 1 ½ cups self-raising flour

100 g / 3 ½ oz / ½ cup butter, cubed

85 g / 3 oz / ⅓ cup caster (superfine) sugar

4 plums, stoned and chopped

1 large egg

75 ml / 2 ½ fl. oz / ⅓ cup whole milk

3 tbsp runny honey

METHOD

1. Preheat the oven to 180°C (160°C fan) / 350F / gas 4 and line a loaf tin with non-stick baking paper.

2. Sieve the flour into a mixing bowl and rub in the butter until it resembles fine breadcrumbs, then stir in the sugar and plums.

3. Beat the egg with the milk and honey then stir it into the dry ingredients until just combined.

4. Scrape the mixture into the loaf tin and bake for 55 minutes or until a skewer inserted comes out clean.

5. Transfer the cake to a wire rack and leave to cool completely.

Chocolate and pistachio cupcakes

MAKES: 12 | PREP TIME: 15 MINUTES | COOKING TIME: 15-20 MINUTES

INGREDIENTS

110 g / 4 oz / ⅔ cup self-raising flour, sifted

2 tbsp cocoa powder

110 g / 4 oz / ½ cup caster (superfine) sugar

110 g / 4 oz / ½ cup butter, softened

2 large eggs

1 tsp almond essence

TO DECORATE:

225 g / 8 oz / 2 ¼ cups icing (confectioner's) sugar

½ tsp almond essence

3 tbsp pistachio nuts, chopped

METHOD

1. Preheat the oven to 190°C (170°C fan) / 375F / gas 5 and line a 12-hole cupcake tin with paper cases.

2. Combine the flour, cocoa, sugar, butter, eggs and almond essence in a bowl and whisk together for 2 minutes or until smooth.

3. Divide the mixture between the paper cases, then transfer the tin to the oven and bake for 15-20 minutes.

4. Test with a wooden toothpick; if it comes out clean, the cakes are done.

5. Transfer the cakes to a wire rack and leave to cool completely before peeling off the papers.

6. To make the icing, sieve the icing sugar into a bowl and add the almond essence. Stir in enough hot water, drop by drop, to form a spreadable icing and spoon it over the cakes.

7. Sprinkle with chopped pistachios and leave the icing to set.

Chocolate chip cupcakes

MAKES: 12 | PREP TIME: 10 MINUTES | COOKING TIME: 15-20 MINUTES

INGREDIENTS

110 g / 4 oz / ⅔ cup self-raising flour, sifted

110 g / 4 oz / ½ cup caster (superfine) sugar

110 g / 4 oz / ½ cup butter, softened

2 large eggs

1 tsp vanilla extract

TO DECORATE:

110 g / 4 oz / ½ cup butter, softened

225 g / 8 oz / 2 ¼ cups icing (confectioner's) sugar

2 tbsp milk

3 tbsp large chocolate chips

METHOD

1. Preheat the oven to 190°C (170°C fan) / 375F / gas 5 and line a 12-hole cupcake tin with paper cases.

2. Combine the flour, sugar, butter, eggs and vanilla extract in a bowl and whisk together for 2 minutes or until smooth.

3. Divide the mixture between the paper cases, transfer the tin to the oven and bake for 15–20 minutes.

4. Test with a wooden toothpick; if it comes out clean, the cakes are done. If not, return the cakes to the oven for another 5 minutes.

5. Transfer the cakes to a wire rack and leave to cool completely.

6. Meanwhile, to make the buttercream, beat the butter with a wooden spoon until fluffy and then gradually beat in the icing sugar, followed by the milk until the buttercream is smooth.

7. Once the cakes are completely cool, spread a thin layer of buttercream over each cake then press 3-4 large chocolate chips onto each one.

8. Leave the icing to set before serving.

Raspberry and coconut cake

SERVES: 8-10 | PREP TIME: 15 MINUTES | COOKING TIME: 45 MINUTES

INGREDIENTS

225 g / 8 oz / 1 cup butter, softened

225 g / 8 oz / 1 cup caster (superfine) sugar

4 large eggs, beaten

225 g/ 4 ½ oz / 1 ½ cups self-raising flour

100 g / 3 ½ oz / 1 cup desiccated coconut

150 g / 5 ½ oz / 1 cup raspberries

3 tbsp toasted coconut flakes

METHOD

1. Preheat the oven to 180°C (160°C fan) / 350F / gas 4 and grease and line a 23 cm round cake tin with greaseproof paper.

2. Cream the butter and sugar together until well whipped, then gradually whisk in the eggs, beating well after each addition.

3. Fold in the flour, desiccated coconut and raspberries, then scrape the mixture into the tin. Sprinkle over the coconut flakes.

4. Bake the cake for 45 minutes, until a skewer inserted in the centre comes out clean.

5. Transfer the cake to a wire rack and leave to cool.

Mini chocolate mousse cakes

MAKES: 6 | PREP TIME: 30 MINUTES | COOKING TIME: 30 MINUTES

CHILLING TIME: 2 HOURS

INGREDIENTS

175 g / 6 oz / ¾ cup unsalted butter, softened

175 g / 6 oz / ¾ cup caster (superfine) sugar

3 large eggs

150 g / 5 ¼ oz / 1 cup self-raising flour

50 g / 1 ¾ oz / ¼ cup cocoa powder

1 tsp baking powder

1 tsp vanilla extract

FOR THE MOUSSE:

150 g / 5 ¼ oz dark chocolate

5 eggs, whites only

50 g / 1 ¾ oz / ¼ cup caster (superfine) sugar

FOR THE TOPPING:

100 g / 3 ½ oz dark chocolate, broken into pieces

100 ml / 3 ½ fl. oz / ½ cup double (heavy) cream

3 strawberries, halved

METHOD

1. Preheat the oven to 180°C (160°C fan) / 350F / gas 4 and grease and line a 20cm baking tray.

2. Beat together the butter and sugar. Whisk in the eggs individually, before adding the rest of the ingredients. Mix until a batter forms.

3. Pour into the baking tray and bake in the oven for 25 minutes until springy when lightly pressed and a skewer inserted into the centre comes out clean. Remove from the oven to cool.

4. Using 6 circular moulds, press them into the sponge base and remove onto greaseproof paper with the cake inside.

5. For the mousse, melt the chocolate. Whisk the egg whites and sugar together until silky and soft peaks form. Whisk a third of the mixture into the melted chocolate until thick, then fold in the rest.

6. Spoon the mixture into the moulds and place in the fridge to chill for at least 2 hours or until set, then remove from the moulds.

7. For the topping, heat the cream in a saucepan until simmering. Transfer to a bowl with the chocolate and whisk until combined and shiny. Pour over the cakes and top with the strawberries.

Summer fruit loaf cake

SERVES: 8 | PREP TIME: 15 MINUTES | COOKING TIME: 45 MINUTES

INGREDIENTS

225 g / 8oz / 1 ½ cups self-raising flour

100 g / 3 ½ oz / ½ cup butter, cubed

85 g / 3 oz / ⅓ cup caster (superfine) sugar

100 g / 3 ½ oz / ⅓ cup raspberries

100 g / 3 ½ oz / ⅔ cup blackberries

55 g / 2 oz / ⅔ cup redcurrants

1 large egg

75 ml / 2 ½ fl. oz / ⅓ cup whole milk

METHOD

1. Preheat the oven to 180°C (160°C fan) / 350F / gas 4 and line a loaf tin with non-stick baking paper.

2. Sieve the flour into a mixing bowl and rub in the butter until it resembles fine breadcrumbs then stir in the sugar and fruit.

3. Lightly beat the egg with the milk and stir it into the dry ingredients until just combined.

4. Scrape the mixture into the loaf tin and bake for 45 minutes or until a skewer inserted in the centre comes out clean.

5. Transfer the cake to a wire rack and leave to cool completely.

Orange drizzle cake

SERVES: 10 | PREP TIME: 10 MINUTES | COOKING TIME: 35-40 MINUTES

INGREDIENTS

150 g / 5 ½ oz / 1 cup self-raising flour

150 g / 5 ½ oz / ⅔ cup caster (superfine) sugar

150 g / 5 ½ oz / ⅔ cup butter

3 eggs

1 tsp baking powder

1 tbsp orange zest

2 tbsp orange juice

FOR THE DRIZZLE:

100 g / 3 ½ oz / ½ cup caster (superfine) sugar

50 ml / 1 ¾ fl. oz / ¼ cup orange juice

METHOD

1. Preheat the oven to 180°C (160°C fan) / 350F / gas 4 and grease and line a 20 cm round cake tin.

2. Put all of the cake ingredients in a large mixing bowl and whisk them together with an electric whisk for 4 minutes or until pale and well whipped.

3. Scrape the mixture into the tin and level the top with a spatula.

4. Bake for 35–40 minutes. While the cake is cooking, stir the caster sugar with the orange juice until dissolved.

5. The cake is ready when a toothpick inserted in the centre comes out clean. Spoon the orange drizzle all over the surface and leave it to cool in the tin.

Chocolate coconut cake

SERVES: 8-10 | PREP TIME: 30 MINUTES | COOKING TIME: 45 MINUTES

INGREDIENTS

FOR THE COCONUT:

2 egg whites

75 g / 2 ½ oz / ⅓ cup caster (superfine) sugar

2 tbsp cornflour (cornstarch)

200 g / 7 oz / 2 cups desiccated coconut

FOR THE CAKE:

175 g / 6 oz / ¾ cup unsalted butter, softened

175 g / 6 oz / ¾ cup caster (superfine) sugar

3 large eggs

150 g / 5 ¼ oz / 1 cup self-raising flour

50 g / 1 ¾ oz / ¼ cup cocoa powder

1 tsp baking powder

50 g / 1 ¾ oz coconut, thinly sliced

METHOD

1. Whisk the egg whites until soft peaks form, then add the sugar and whisk until silken. Mix through the cornflour and coconut until thick. Set aside.

2. Preheat the oven to 180°C (160°C fan) / 350F / gas 4 and grease and line a 18cm round cake tin.

3. Beat together the butter and sugar until creamy. Whisk in the eggs, then add the flour, cocoa and baking powder. Mix until a batter forms. Pour half the cake batter into the prepared tin before dotting around the coconut mixture. Pour over the remaining cake batter.

4. Bake in the oven for 45 minutes until risen. The cake is ready when a skewer inserted into the centre of the cake comes out clean.

5. Remove from the oven to cool and sprinkle with the thinly sliced coconut shards.

Ginger and nut cupcakes

MAKES: 12 | PREP TIME: 30 MINUTES | COOKING TIME: 20 MINUTES

INGREDIENTS

200 g / 7 oz / 1 ¼ cups light brown sugar

200 g / 7 oz / 1 ⅓ cups self-raising flour

1 tsp bicarbonate of (baking) soda

1 tsp ground ginger

2 eggs

150 ml / 5 ¼ fl. oz / ⅔ cup sunflower oil

50 g / 1 ¾ oz ginger root, peeled and grated

100 g / 3 ½ oz / ¾ cup hazelnuts (cob nuts), chopped

100 g / 3 ½ oz / ½ cup unsalted butter, softened

300 g / 10 ½ oz / 2 cups cream cheese

100 g / 3 ½ oz / 1 cup icing (confectioner's) sugar

1 tsp vanilla extract

1 lemon, zest

METHOD

1. Preheat the oven to 180°C (160°C fan) / 350F / gas 4 and line a 12-hole muffin tin with cases.

2. In bowl, mix together the first four ingredients. In a separate bowl, whisk together the eggs and oil until frothy. Mix into the dry ingredients to form a smooth batter.

3. Fold the ginger root and 75 g of the hazelnuts into the mixture before spooning into the cases.

4. Bake in the oven for approximately 20 minutes until springy and a skewer inserted into the centre of a cake comes out clean. Remove to cool on a wire rack.

5. Beat together the butter, cream cheese, icing sugar, vanilla and lemon zest. Spoon the icing onto the cooled cupcakes and sprinkle with the remaining nuts.

Vanilla cupcakes

MAKES: 12 | PREP TIME: 15 MINUTES | COOKING TIME: 15 MINUTES

INGREDIENTS

FOR THE CAKES:

150 g / 5 ¼ oz / ⅔ cup unsalted butter, softened

150 g / 5 ¼ oz / ⅔ cup caster (superfine) sugar

2 free-range eggs, beaten

1 tsp vanilla extract

150 g / 5 ¼ oz / 1 cup self-raising flour

2 tbsp milk

FOR THE ICING:

120 g / 4 ¼ oz / ½ cup unsalted butter, softened

220 g / 7 ¾ oz / 2 ¼ cups icing (confectioner's) sugar

1 tsp vanilla extract

50 g / 1 ¾ oz colourful sugar cake sprinkles

METHOD

1. Preheat the oven to 180°C (160°C fan) / 350F / gas 4 and line a muffin tray with cases.

2. Cream together the butter and sugar using an electric whisk. Beat in the eggs and vanilla extract followed by the flour and enough of the milk to form a smooth batter.

3. Spoon into the prepared cases to around halfway. Bake in the oven for 15 minutes until a skewer inserted into the centre of a cake comes out clean. Remove to cool on a wire rack.

4. Cream together the butter, icing sugar and vanilla extract. Add a splash of milk if the mixture is a little stiff. Spoon into a piping bag with a star nozzle and top the cooled cakes with the icing before adding the cake sprinkles.

Chocolate loaf cake

SERVES: 8 | PREP TIME: 20 MINUTES | COOKING TIME: 45 MINUTES

INGREDIENTS

225 g / 8 oz / 1 cup butter, softened

225 g / 8 oz / 1 cup caster (superfine) sugar

4 large eggs, beaten

225 g / 8 oz / 1 ½ cups self-raising flour

2 tbsp unsweetened cocoa powder

100 g / 3 ½ oz milk chocolate, grated

METHOD

1. Preheat the oven to 180°C (160°C fan) / 350F / gas 4 and grease and line a loaf tin with greaseproof paper.

2. Cream together the butter and sugar until well whipped, then gradually whisk in the eggs, beating well after each addition.

3. Sift over the flour and cocoa powder and fold in with the grated chocolate.

4. Scrape the mixture into the tin and bake for 45 minutes or until a skewer inserted in the centre comes out clean.

5. Turn the loaf out onto a wire rack and leave to cool.

111

Chocolate peanut cupcakes

MAKES: 12 | PREP TIME: 30 MINUTES | COOKING TIME: 20 MINUTES

INGREDIENTS

200 g / 7 oz / 1 ¼ cups light brown sugar

200 g / 7 oz / 1 ⅓ cups self-raising flour

1 tsp bicarbonate of (baking) soda

100 g / 3 ½ oz / ⅔ cup cocoa powder

2 eggs

150 ml / 5 ¼ fl. oz / ⅔ cup sunflower oil

100 g / 3 ½ oz peanut butter

100 g / 3 ½ oz / ½ cup unsalted butter, softened

300 g / 10 ½ oz / 3 cups icing (confectioner's) sugar

METHOD

1. Preheat the oven to 180°C (160°C fan) / 350F / gas 4 and line a 12-hole muffin tin with cases.

2. In a mixing bowl, combine the first three ingredients and half the cocoa. In a separate bowl, whisk the eggs and oil until frothy. Mix into the dry ingredients to form a batter.

3. Spoon the batter into the prepared cases and bake in the oven for around 20 minutes until risen and a skewer inserted into the centre of a cake comes out clean. Remove to cool.

4. Beat the peanut butter with 25 g of the butter and half the icing sugar until light and creamy.

5. In a separate bowl, mix the remaining butter and cocoa and the icing sugar until creamy. To decorate, pipe some of the peanut mixture into the centre of each cake, pushing slightly into the cake to fill it. Then pipe the chocolate mixture around the peanut topping.

Semolina coconut cake

SERVES: 8-10 | PREP TIME: 20 MINUTES | COOKING TIME: 40 MINUTES

INGREDIENTS

225 g / 8 oz / 1 cup caster (superfine) sugar

225 g / 8 oz / 1 cup unsalted butter, softened

3 eggs, separated

1 tsp almond essence

200 g / 7 oz / 2 cups desiccated coconut

200 g / 7 oz / 1 ½ cups semolina (cream of wheat)

1 tsp baking powder

a pinch of salt

50 g / 1 ¾ oz sugared almonds

METHOD

1. Preheat the oven to 180°C (160°C fan) / 350F / gas 4 and grease and line a 20cm square baking tin.

2. In a stand mixer, cream together the sugar and butter until pale and fluffy. Add the egg yolks one at a time, followed by the almond essence, and combine, then fold in the coconut, semolina, baking powder and salt.

3. Whisk the egg whites until soft peaks form and fold into the batter until fully combined.

4. Pour the batter into the prepared tin and dot with the sugared almonds at regular intervals. Place into the oven and cook for 40 minutes until golden brown and a skewer inserted into the centre of the cake comes out clean.

5. Remove to cool before cutting into squares.

Chocolate cupcakes with raspberry

MAKES: 12 | PREP TIME: 30 MINUTES | COOKING TIME: 20 MINUTES

INGREDIENTS

200 g / 7 oz / 1 ¼ cups light brown sugar

200 g / 7 oz / 1 ⅓ cups self-raising flour

1 tsp bicarbonate of (baking) soda

100 g / 3 ½ oz / ⅔ cup cocoa powder

2 large eggs

150 ml / 5 ¼ fl. oz / ⅔ cup sunflower oil

FOR THE ICING:

125 g / 4 ¼ oz / ½ cup unsalted butter, softened

300 g / 10 ½ oz / 3 cups icing (confectioner's) sugar

1 tbsp double (heavy) cream

1 tsp vanilla extract

75 g / 2 ½ oz / ½ cup raspberries

12 decorative chocolate or sugar hearts

METHOD

1. Preheat the oven to 180°C (160°C fan) / 350F / gas 4 and line a 12-hole muffin tin with cases.

2. In a large mixing bowl, combine the sugar, flour, bicarbonate of soda and half the cocoa. In a separate bowl, whisk together the eggs and oil until frothy. Mix into the dry ingredients to form a smooth batter.

3. Spoon the batter into the prepared cases and bake in the oven for around 20 minutes until risen and a skewer inserted into the centre of a cake comes out clean. Remove to cool.

4. Beat the butter until light and gradually add the icing sugar, beating until you have a smooth and creamy mixture, adding the cream and vanilla extract midway through.

5. Place the raspberries into a blender and blend to a pulp. Pass through a sieve into a clean bowl. Mix half of the buttercream into the raspberry before placing the toppings into a piping bag and piping onto the cooled cakes. Top with a decorative heart.

Peach loaf cake

SERVES: 8 | PREP TIME: 20 MINUTES | COOKING TIME: 45 MINUTES

INGREDIENTS

200 g / 7 oz / ¾ cup caster (superfine) sugar

250 g / 9 oz / 1 ¼ cups unsalted butter, softened

1 tsp vanilla extract

200 g / 7 oz / 1 ⅓ cups plain (all-purpose) flour

2 tsp baking powder

100 g / 3 ½ oz / 1 cup ground almonds

a pinch of salt

4 eggs

200 g / 7 oz peach slices

METHOD

1. Preheat the oven to 200°C (180°C fan) / 400F / gas 6 and grease and line a loaf tin.

2. Cream together the sugar, butter and vanilla extract in a stand mixer until pale and fluffy. Add the flour, baking powder, ground almonds and salt and mix through. Add the eggs one at a time and continue to mix on a low speed for a couple of minutes until smooth.

3. Pour into the prepared loaf tin and push the peach slices into the cake at regular intervals.

4. Place the cake into the centre of the oven and bake for around 45 minutes until risen and a skewer inserted into the centre of the cake comes out clean.

5. Remove to cool before turning out onto a wire rack to cool completely.

Mandarin cake

MAKES: 12 | PREP TIME: 20 MINUTES | COOKING TIME: 30 MINUTES

INGREDIENTS

300 g / 10 ½ oz / 2 ⅓ cups plain (all-purpose) flour

2 tbsp baking powder

a pinch of salt

200 g / 7 oz / ¾ cup caster (superfine) sugar

3 free-range eggs

80 ml / 2 ¾ fl. oz / ⅓ cup vegetable oil

1 tsp vanilla extract

300 g / 10 ½ oz mandarin segments in syrup

200 ml / 7 fl. oz / ¾ cup double (heavy) cream

100 g / 3 ½ oz / 1 cup icing (confectioner's) sugar

50 g / 1 ¾ oz smooth marmalade

METHOD

1. Preheat the oven to 200°C (180°C fan) / 400F / gas 6 and grease and line a 9 inch square cake tin.

2. Place the flour, baking powder, salt and sugar into a large mixing bowl.

3. Whisk together the egg, oil, vanilla extract and mandarin segments with half of the syrup. This should break down the fruit into smaller pieces.

4. Make a well in the centre of the dry ingredients and pour in the wet. Whisk to incorporate and to get air into the mixture.

5. Pour the batter into the prepared tin and bake for 30 minutes until a skewer inserted into the centre of the cake comes out clean. Remove to cool.

6. Whisk together the cream and icing sugar until light and fluffy. Once the cake has cooled spread a layer of the cream mixture on top. Put the rest into a piping bag and pipe small swirls at regular intervals. Top with a small amount of marmalade and cut out into cubes.

118

Bundt cakes with lime and raspberries

MAKES: 6 | PREP TIME: 20 MINUTES | COOKING TIME: 20 MINUTES

INGREDIENTS

175 g / 6 oz / 1 ¼ cups plain (all-purpose) flour

150 g / 5 ¼ oz / ⅔ cup caster (superfine) sugar

1 tsp baking powder

150 ml / 5 ¼ fl. oz / ⅔ cup milk

2 limes, juice and zest

2 eggs, beaten

75 g / 2 ½ oz unsalted butter, melted

200 ml / 7 fl. oz / ¾ cup double (heavy) cream

100 g / 3 ½ oz / ⅔ cup raspberries

sprigs of mint, to garnish

lime slices, to garnish

METHOD

1. Preheat the oven to 160°C (140°C fan) / 325F / gas 3 and grease 6 mini bundt cake tins.

2. Combine the flour, sugar and baking powder in a large mixing bowl. In a separate bowl, combine the milk, lime juice and zest, eggs and butter.

3. Make a well in the centre of the dry mixture and mix gradually with the wet until smooth.

4. Spoon into the tins and bake for 20 minutes until risen and golden. Remove and cool in the tins, then turn out to cool completely.

5. To decorate, whip the cream until thickened and spoon over the cakes. Place the raspberries on top and garnish with mint and lime slices.

Strawberry cupcakes

MAKES : 12 | PREP TIME: 15 MINUTES | COOKING TIME: 15 MINUTES

INGREDIENTS

FOR THE CAKES

175 g / 6 oz / ¾ cup unsalted butter, softened

175 g / 6 oz / ¾ cup caster (superfine) sugar

2 free-range eggs, beaten

175 g / 6 oz / 1 ¼ cup self-raising flour

2 tbsp milk

150 g / 5 ¼ oz fresh strawberries

FOR THE ICING:

500 ml / 17 fl. oz / 2 cups double (heavy) cream

220 g / 7 ¾ oz / 2 ¼ cups icing (confectioner's) sugar

1 tsp vanilla extract

METHOD

1. Preheat the oven to 180°C (160°C fan) / 350F / gas 4 and line a muffin tray with cases.

2. Cream together the butter and sugar using an electric whisk. Beat in the eggs, flour and enough of the milk to form a smooth batter. Set aside 12 strawberries for decoration. Chop the remaining ones, then fold through the batter.

3. Spoon into the prepared cases to around halfway. Bake in the oven for 15 minutes until a skewer inserted into the centre of a cake comes out clean. Remove to cool on a wire rack.

4. Whip the cream then add the icing sugar and vanilla extract. Continue to whip until creamy before piping onto the cakes and topping with the reserved fruit.

121

Easter cupcakes

SERVES: 12 | PREP TIME: 10 MINUTES | COOKING TIME: 15 MINUTES

INGREDIENTS

175 g / 6 oz / ¾ cup unsalted butter, softened

175 g / 6 oz / ¾ cup caster (superfine) sugar

2 free-range eggs, beaten

175 g / 6 oz / 1 ¼ cup self-raising flour

2 tbsp milk

FOR THE ICING:

120 g / 4 ¼ oz / ½ cup unsalted butter, softened

175 g / 6 oz / 1 ¾ cups icing (confectioner's) sugar

50 g / 1 ¾ oz / ¼ cup cocoa powder

chocolate eggs and sugar flowers, to decorate

METHOD

1. Preheat the oven to 180°C (160°C fan) / 350F / gas 4 and line a muffin tray with cases.

2. Cream the butter and sugar using an electric whisk. Beat in the eggs and flour and enough of the milk to form a smooth batter with a thick consistency.

3. Spoon into the prepared cases and bake in the oven for 15 minutes until springy and a skewer inserted into the centre of a cake comes out clean. Remove to cool on a wire rack.

4. Beat together the butter, icing sugar and cocoa until smooth. Place into a piping bag with a small star nozzle and pipe nests on top of the cakes. Fill the icing nests with chocolate eggs and sugar flowers.

Almond loaf cake

SERVES: 8 | PREP TIME: 20 MINUTES | COOKING TIME: 45 MINUTES

INGREDIENTS

125 g / 4 ¼ oz / ¾ cup self-raising flour

100 g / 3 ½ oz / 1 cup ground almonds

110 g / 3 ¾ oz / ½ cup unsalted butter

110 g / 3 ¾ oz / ½ cup caster (superfine) sugar

1 egg, beaten

75 ml / 2 ½ fl. oz / ⅓ cup milk

1 tsp vanilla extract

75 g / 2 ½ oz / 1 cup flaked (slivered) almonds

METHOD

1. Preheat the oven to 200°C (180°C fan) / 400F / gas 6 and line a loaf tin with greaseproof paper.

2. In a bowl, rub the flour, ground almonds and butter together until you achieve breadcrumb consistency. Mix through the sugar.

3. Combine the egg, milk and vanilla extract in a jug and whisk. Add to the mixing bowl and stir until you have a smooth batter.

4. Pour into the prepared tin and top with the flaked almonds. Bake in the oven for approximately 45 minutes or until a skewer inserted into the centre comes out clean.

5. Remove from the oven to cool completely before serving.

Cherry loaf cake

SERVES: 8 | PREP TIME: 20 MINUTES | COOKING TIME: 45 MINUTES

INGREDIENTS

200 g / 7 oz / ¾ cup caster (superfine) sugar

250 g / 9 oz / 1 ¼ cups unsalted butter, softened

1 tsp vanilla extract

200 g / 7 oz / 1 ⅓ cups plain (all-purpose) flour

2 tsp baking powder

100 g / 3 ½ oz / 1 cup ground almonds

a pinch of salt

4 eggs

150 g / 5 ¼ oz fresh cherries, halved and pitted

METHOD

1. Preheat the oven to 200°C (180°C fan) / 400F / gas 6 and grease and line a loaf tin.

2. Cream together the sugar, butter and vanilla extract in a stand mixer. Add the flour, baking powder, ground almonds and salt and mix through. Add the eggs and continue to mix on a low speed for a couple of minutes until smooth. Fold in the prepared cherries.

3. Pour into the prepared loaf tin and place the cake into the centre of the oven and bake for around 45 minutes until risen and a skewer inserted into the centre comes out clean.

4. Remove to cool before turning out onto a wire rack to cool completely.

Coconut cupcakes

MAKES: 24 | PREP TIME: 15 MINUTES | COOKING TIME: 20 MINUTES

INGREDIENTS

250 g / 9 oz / 1 ¼ cups unsalted butter

250 g / 9 oz / 1 ¼ cups caster (superfine) sugar

250 g / 9 oz / 1 ⅔ cups self-raising flour

a pinch of salt

4 free-range eggs

75 ml / 2 ½ fl. oz / ⅓ cup milk

1 tsp vanilla extract

100 g / 3 ½ oz / 1 cup desiccated coconut

400 ml / 13 ½ fl. oz / 1 ⅔ cups double (heavy) cream

300 g / 10 ½ oz / 3 cups icing (confectioner's) sugar

METHOD

1. Preheat the oven to 180°C (160°C fan) / 350F / gas 4 and line two 12-hole muffin trays.

2. Cream together the butter and sugar in a stand mixer until pale and creamy.

3. Add the flour, salt and then the eggs, one at a time and mixing fully after each addition. Finally, mix in the milk, vanilla and coconut.

4. Spoon into the cases and bake in for 20 minutes until golden and springy. Remove to cool.

5. Whisk the double cream until it starts to thicken, sift the icing sugar into the cream and mix thoroughly until smooth. Pipe the cream on top of the cakes and decorate with additional sugar sprinkles if desired.

Lime sponge cake

SERVES: 8 | PREP TIME: **15 MINUTES** | COOKING TIME: **30 MINUTES**

INGREDIENTS

150 g / 5 ¼ oz / ⅔ cup unsalted butter, softened

150 g / 5 ¼ oz / ⅔ cup caster (superfine) sugar

200 g / 7 oz / 1 ⅓ cups self-raising flour

1 tsp baking powder

3 large eggs

2 tbsp milk

5 limes

250 g / 9 oz / 2 ½ cups icing (confectioner's) sugar

METHOD

1. Preheat the oven to 180°C (160°C fan) / 350F / gas 4. Grease and line a 20cm spring-form cake tin.

2. Place the butter, sugar, flour, baking powder, eggs and milk into a stand mixer with a beater attachment. Mix for a few minutes, add the zest and juice from two limes and mix through.

3. Pour into the prepared tin and bake for around 30 minutes until golden and a skewer inserted into the centre of the cake comes out clean. Remove to a wire rack to cool.

4. To make the icing, juice and zest the remaining limes. Mix the juice and icing sugar to make a thick yet slightly runny glaze. Pour over the cake and scatter the lime zest over the cake.

Almond caramel cakes

MAKES: 12 | PREP TIME: 20 MINUTES | COOKING TIME: 20 MINUTES

INGREDIENTS

350 g / 12 oz / 2 cups light brown sugar

225 g / 8 oz / 1 ½ cups self-raising flour

1 tsp bicarbonate of (baking) soda

2 eggs

150 ml / 5 ¼ fl. oz / ⅔ cup sunflower oil

100 g / 3 ½ oz almond butter

200 g / 7 oz / ¾ cup unsalted butter, softened

300 g / 10 ½ oz / 3 cups icing (confectioner's) sugar

1 tsp vanilla extract

1 tbsp golden syrup

2 tsp sea salt flakes

100 ml / 3 ½ fl. oz / ½ cup double (heavy) cream

100 g / 3 ½ oz sugared almonds, lightly chopped

METHOD

1. Preheat the oven to 180°C (160°C fan) / 350F / gas 4 and line a 12-hole muffin tin with cases.

2. In a mixing bowl, combine 200 g of the sugar, flour and bicarbonate of soda. In a separate bowl, whisk the eggs and oil until frothy. Mix into the dry ingredients to form a smooth batter.

3. Spoon the batter into the cases. Bake in the oven for 20 minutes until a skewer inserted into the centre of a cake comes out clean. Remove to cool.

4. Beat the almond butter with half of the butter and all of the icing sugar until light and creamy, then mix through the vanilla extract.

5. In a pan, heat the remaining brown sugar, butter and golden syrup until you have a thick caramel. Add the salt and double cream. Mix until pale.

6. Pipe the almond butter icing on top of the cakes before dotting with chopped almonds. Spoon over some of the salted caramel sauce to finish.

Chocolate butter cake

SERVES: 12 | PREP TIME: 25 MINUTES | COOKING TIME: 45 MINUTES

INGREDIENTS

75 g / 2 ½ oz / ½ cup cocoa powder

50 ml / 1 ¾ fl. oz / ¼ cup boiling water

125 g / 4 ¼ oz / ½ cup unsalted butter, softened

300 g / 10 ½ oz / 1 ⅓ cups caster (superfine) sugar

3 large free-range eggs

150 ml / 5 ¼ fl. oz / ⅔ cup milk

200 g / 7 oz / 1 ⅓ cups self-raising flour

1 tsp baking powder

150 g / 5 ¼ oz / 1 ¼ cups chopped almonds

200 g / 7 oz chocolate

100 ml / 3 ½ fl. oz / ½ cup double (heavy) cream

1 tsp vanilla extract

chocolate twirls, to decorate

METHOD

1. Preheat the oven to 180°C (160°C fan) / 350F / gas 4 and grease and line a 23cm square baking tray.

2. Mix the cocoa with the boiling water, then stir in the butter until smooth. Add the sugar, eggs, milk, flour and baking powder and continue to mix into a smooth batter. Fold two-thirds of the almonds through the mixture.

3. Pour the batter into the prepared tin and bake in the oven for 30 minutes until risen and starting to come away from the edges of the tin. Remove and allow to cool in the tin for 10 minutes before transferring to a wire rack to cool completely.

4. Break the chocolate into a saucepan and gently heat until warm. Remove from the heat and pour in the cream and vanilla extract and mix to form a smooth ganache.

5. Pour the icing over the cake and spread evenly over the whole sponge. Sprinkle the top of the cake with the remaining nuts and twirls of milk chocolate.

Cook's Corner

Muffins and other bakes
Sweet treats

Millionaire's shortbread

MAKES: 9 | PREP TIME: 4 HOURS 30 MINUTES | COOKING TIME: 20 MINUTES

INGREDIENTS

FOR THE SHORTBREAD:

230 g / 8 oz / 1 ½ cups plain (all-purpose) flour

2 tbsp cocoa powder

75 g / 2 ½ oz / ⅓ cup caster (superfine) sugar

150 g / 5 oz / ⅔ cup butter, cubed

FOR THE TOPPING:

1 can condensed milk

200 g / 7 oz milk chocolate

METHOD

1. To make the caramel layer, put the unopened can of condensed milk in a pan of water. Simmer for 3 hours, then leave the can to cool.

2. Preheat the oven to 180°C (160°C fan) / 350F / gas 4 and line a 20 cm square cake tin with greaseproof paper.

3. Mix the flour, cocoa and caster sugar in a bowl, then rub in the butter. Knead until the mixture forms a dough then press it evenly into the bottom of the tin.

4. Bake the shortbread for 15 minutes. Leave to cool. Open the condensed milk. Beat until smooth. Spread it over the shortbread. Chill for 1 hour.

5. Melt the chocolate in a microwave. Spread it over the caramel. Chill in the fridge for 30 minutes.

Blueberry tartlets

MAKES: 6 | PREP TIME: 1 HOUR | COOKING TIME: 35-40 MINUTES

INGREDIENTS

200 g / 7 oz blueberries

FOR THE PASTRY:

100 g / 3 ½ oz / ⅓ cup butter, cubed

200 g / 7 oz / 1 ⅓ cups plain (all-purpose) flour

1 egg, beaten

FOR THE CUSTARD:

2 large egg yolks

55 g / 2 oz caster (superfine) sugar

2 tsp cornflour (cornstarch)

225 ml / 8 fl. oz / 1 cup whole milk

METHOD

1. To make the pastry, rub the butter into the flour. Add a little cold water to bind. Chill for 30 minutes in the fridge, wrapped in clingfilm.

2. Preheat the oven to 200°C (180°C fan) / 400F / gas 6. Meanwhile, roll out the pastry on a floured surface and use it to line 6 tartlet cases.

3. Prick the pastry with a fork, line with greaseproof paper and fill with baking beans or rice. Bake for 10 minutes, then remove the paper and baking beans.

4. Brush the inside of the pastry cases with beaten egg and cook for another 8 minutes to crisp.

5. Whisk the custard ingredients together in a jug and three-quarters fill the pastry cases. Bake the tarts for 15-20 minutes. Leave the tartlets to cool completely before topping with the blueberries.

133

Black sesame tuiles

MAKES: 18 | PREP TIME: 45 MINUTES | COOKING TIME: 8-10 MINUTES

INGREDIENTS

110 g / 4 oz / ⅔ cup plain (all-purpose) flour

110 g / 4 oz / ½ cup caster (superfine) sugar

2 large egg whites

110 g / 4 oz / ½ cup butter, melted

2 tbsp black sesame seeds

METHOD

1. Beat together the flour, sugar and egg whites until smooth, then beat in the melted butter and sesame seeds.

2. Refrigerate for 30 minutes.

3. Preheat the oven to 180°C (160°C fan) / 350F / gas 4 and oil 2 large baking trays.

4. Spoon teaspoonfuls of the mixture onto the baking trays and spread out with the back of the spoon to make 10 cm circles.

5. Bake the tuiles for 8-10 minutes then lift them off the trays with a palette knife and drape over a rolling pin while still soft. Leave to cool and harden.

Milk chocolate fondants

MAKES: 6 | PREP TIME: 50 MINUTES | COOKING TIME: 8 MINUTES

INGREDIENTS

2 tbsp unsweetened cocoa powder

150 g / 6 oz milk chocolate, chopped

150 g / 6 oz / ⅔ cup butter, chopped

85 g / 3 oz / ⅓ cup caster (superfine) sugar

3 large eggs

3 extra egg yolks

1 tbsp plain (all-purpose) flour

METHOD

1. Oil 6 pudding basins. Dust the insides with cocoa.

2. Melt the chocolate, butter and sugar together in a saucepan, stirring to dissolve the sugar.

3. Leave to cool a little, then beat in the eggs and egg yolks and fold in the flour.

4. Divide the mixture between the pudding basins and chill them for 30 minutes.

5. Preheat the oven to 180°C (160°C fan) / 350F / gas 4 and put a baking tray in to heat.

6. Transfer the fondants to the heated baking tray and bake in the oven for 8 minutes.

7. Leave the fondants to cool for 2 minutes, then turn them out of their moulds and serve immediately.

Rhubarb and custard tart

SERVES: 8 | PREP TIME: 1 HOUR 20 MINUTES | COOKING TIME: 45-55 MINUTES

INGREDIENTS

3 sticks rhubarb, chopped

4 tbsp caster (superfine) sugar

icing (confectioner's) sugar, to dust

FOR THE PASTRY:

200 g / 7 oz / 1 ⅓ cups plain (all-purpose) flour

100 g / 3 ½ oz / ½ cup butter, cubed

FOR THE CUSTARD:

4 large egg yolks

75 g / 2 ½ oz / ⅓ cup caster (superfine) sugar

2 tsp cornflour (cornstarch)

450 ml / 16 fl. oz / 1 ¾ cups whole milk

METHOD

1. Preheat the oven to 200°C (180°C fan) /400F / gas 6. Meanwhile, put the rhubarb in a roasting tin. Sprinkle with sugar and bake for 20 minutes.

2. To make the pastry, rub the butter into the flour and add a little cold water to bind. Chill for 30 minutes, then roll out on a floured surface and spread over a rectangular tart tin.

3. Prick the pastry with a fork, line with baking paper and fill with baking beans or rice. Bake for 10 minutes then remove the paper and baking beans. Cook for another 8 minutes.

4. Whisk together the custard ingredients and pour into the pastry case. Arrange the rhubarb on top.

5. Reduce the oven to 170°C (150°C fan) / 340F / gas 3 and bake for 25-35 minutes until just set.

6. Leave to cool before dusting with icing sugar.

Raspberry sponge squares

MAKES: 12 | PREP TIME: 10 MINUTES | COOKING TIME: 30-35 MINUTES

INGREDIENTS

175 g / 6 oz / 1 ¼ cup self-raising flour

2 tsp baking powder

175 g / 6 oz / ¾ cup caster (superfine) sugar

175 g / 6 oz / ¾ cup butter

3 eggs

200 g / 7 oz / 1 ⅓ cups raspberries

icing (confectioner's) sugar to dust

METHOD

1. Preheat the oven to 180°C (160°C fan) / 350F / gas 4 and grease and line a square cake tin.

2. Put the flour, baking powder, sugar, butter and eggs in a mixing bowl and whisk them together with an electric whisk for 4 minutes.

3. Arrange the raspberries in the bottom of the cake tin and spoon over the cake mixture.

4. Bake for 30-35 minutes. The cake is ready when a toothpick inserted in the centre comes out clean.

5. Transfer the cake to a wire rack to cool completely before dusting with icing sugar and cutting into squares.

137

Hot cross bun loaf

SERVES: 8 | PREP TIME: 3 HOURS | COOKING TIME: 35-40 MINUTES

INGREDIENTS

55 g / 2 oz / ¼ cup butter, cubed

400 g / 14 oz / 2 ⅔ cups strong white bread flour, plus extra for dusting

½ tsp easy-blend dried yeast

4 tbsp caster (superfine) sugar

1 tsp fine sea salt

2 tsp mixed spice

100 g / 3 ½ oz / ½ cup mixed dried fruit

4 tbsp plain (all-purpose) flour

1 egg, beaten

METHOD

1. Rub the butter into the flour. Stir in the yeast, sugar, salt and spice. Stir the dried fruit into 280 ml of warm water, then stir into the dry ingredients.

2. Knead the mixture on an oiled surface for 10 minutes. Leave the dough to rest, covered with an oiled bowl, for 1-2 hours, until doubled in size.

3. Roll the dough into a fat sausage. Turn it 90°. Roll it the other way then tuck the ends under. Transfer to the tin. Leave to prove for 45 minutes.

4. Preheat the oven to 220°C (200°C fan) / 425F / gas 7.

5. Mix the plain flour with a little water to make a paste. Spoon it into a piping bag. Brush the loaf with egg. Pipe the flour mixture on top in crosses.

6. Bake for 35-40 minutes and allow to cool.

Chocolate pear tarte tatin

SERVES: 8 | PREP TIME: 10 MINUTES | COOKING TIME: 20-25 MINUTES

INGREDIENTS

2 tbsp butter

2 tbsp dark brown sugar

6 pears, peeled, cored and halved

250 g / 9 oz all-butter puff pastry

100 g / 3 ½ oz dark chocolate (min. 60% cocoa solids), chopped

METHOD

1. Preheat the oven to 220°C (200°C fan) / 425F / gas 7.

2. Heat the butter and sugar in an ovenproof pan. Add the pears. Cook over a low heat for 5 minutes, turning occasionally, until they start to soften.

3. Arrange the pears in the pan, cut side up.

4. Roll out the pastry on a floured surface and cut out a circle the same size as the frying pan. Lay the pastry over the cooled pears and tuck in the edges. Transfer the pan to the oven. Bake for 25 minutes.

5. Meanwhile, melt the chocolate in a microwave.

6. Using oven gloves, put a plate on top of the frying pan and turn them both over in one smooth movement to unmould the tart.

7. Drizzle the melted chocolate between the pears and serve immediately.

139

Viennese biscuits

MAKES: 20-25 | PREP TIME: 25 MINUTES | COOKING TIME: 15 MINUTES

INGREDIENTS

200 g / 7 oz / ¾ cup unsalted butter, softened

50 g / 1 ¾ oz / ½ cup icing (confectioner's) sugar

200 g / 7 oz / 1 ⅓ cups plain (all-purpose) flour

50 g / 1 ¾ oz / ⅓ cup cornflour (cornstarch)

1 tbsp vanilla extract

METHOD

1. Combine all the ingredients in a large mixing bowl. Mix well to combine before placing in the refrigerator to chill for 20 minutes.

2. Preheat the oven to 180°C (160°C fan) / 350F / gas 4 and line two baking trays with greaseproof paper.

3. Place the biscuit dough into a piping bag with a star nozzle.

4. Pipe the dough onto the prepared baking trays leaving enough space between each to allow for some spread.

5. Bake in the oven for 15 minutes until golden and firm. Remove to cool completely.

Walnut brownies

SERVES: 9 | PREP TIME: 5 MINUTES | COOKING TIME: 35 MINUTES

INGREDIENTS

100 g / 3 ½ oz / ⅔ cup dark chocolate (minimum 85% cocoa solids), chopped

85 g / 3 oz / ¾ cup pure cacao powder

225 g / 8 oz / 1 cup coconut oil

450 g / 1 lb / 2 ½ cups coconut sugar

4 large eggs

8 medjool dates, stoned and very finely chopped

100 g / 3 ½ oz / ⅔ cup buckwheat flour

75 g / 2 ½ oz / ½ cup walnuts, chopped

METHOD

1. Preheat the oven to 160°C (140°C fan) / 325F / gas 3 and oil and line a 20 cm (8 in) square cake tin with greaseproof paper.

2. Melt the chocolate, cacao and coconut oil together in a saucepan, then leave to cool a little.

3. Whisk the sugar, eggs and dates together with an electric whisk for 3 minutes or until very light and creamy.

4. Pour in the chocolate mixture and sieve over the flour, then fold everything together with the walnuts.

5. Scrape the mixture into the tin and bake for 35 minutes until the outside is set, but the centre is still quite soft.

6. Leave the brownie to cool completely before cutting and serving.

141

Apple and walnut tartlets

MAKES: 6 | PREP TIME: 30 MINUTES | COOKING TIME: 20 MINUTES

INGREDIENTS

225 g / 8 oz puff pastry

150 g / 5 ½ oz / 1 ½ cups ground walnuts

150 g / 5 ½ oz / ⅔ cup butter, softened

150 g / 5 ½ oz / ⅔ cup caster (superfine) sugar

2 large eggs

2 tbsp plain (all-purpose) flour

4 eating apples, cored and sliced

4 tbsp runny honey

2 tbsp chopped walnuts

clotted cream or ice cream, to serve

METHOD

1. Preheat the oven to 200°C (180°C fan) / 400F / gas 6.

2. Roll out the pastry on a floured surface and use it to line 6 round loose-bottomed tartlet cases.

3. Prick the pastry with a fork, line with greaseproof paper and fill with baking beans or rice. Bake for 10 minutes then remove the paper and baking beans.

4. Whisk together the ground walnuts, butter, sugar, eggs and flour until smoothly whipped, then spoon the mixture into the pastry case.

5. Arrange the apple slices on top and bake for 20 minutes, until the pastry is crisp underneath.

6. Heat the honey until liquid and stir in the walnuts, then drizzle it over the hot tarts.

7. Serve warm with clotted cream or ice cream.

Palmier biscuits

MAKES: 15-20 | PREP TIME: 20 MINUTES | COOKING TIME: 20 MINUTES

INGREDIENTS

320 g / 11 oz puff pastry sheet, all butter

200 g / 7 oz / ¾ cup demerara sugar

2 tsp cinnamon

METHOD

1. Preheat the oven to 200°C (180°C fan) / 400F / gas 6 and line a baking tray with greaseproof paper.

2. Roll out the pastry to an even 1 cm thickness.

3. Sprinkle the surface of the pastry with half the sugar and most of the cinnamon before gently rolling into the pastry with a rolling pin. Lie the pastry so that the longest edge is in front of you and fold the shorter edges to meet in the middle.

4. Sprinkle with the remaining cinnamon and half the remaining sugar. Fold in half so that the two rounded edges are together and the pastry is in a sausage shape.

5. Cut across the pastry to 2 cm thickness so that you have several heart-shaped biscuits. Place onto the prepared tray. Sprinkle with remaining sugar. Place in the fridge to chill for 10 minutes.

6. Bake in the oven for 20 minutes until golden. Leave to cool on the tray before eating.

Lemon and almond shortbread biscuits

MAKES: 15-20 | PREP TIME: 20 MINUTES | COOKING TIME: 15-20 MINUTES

INGREDIENTS

175 g / 6 oz / 1 cup plain (all-purpose) flour

55 g / 2 oz / ½ cup ground almonds

75 g / 2 ½ oz / ⅓ cup caster (superfine) sugar

150 g / 5 oz / ⅔ cup butter, cubed

1 lemon, zest finely grated

50 g / 1 ¾ oz / ¼ cup granulated sugar

METHOD

1. Preheat the oven to 180°C (160°C fan) 350F / gas 4 and line a baking tray with greaseproof paper.

2. Mix together the flour, ground almonds and caster sugar in a bowl, then rub in the butter and lemon zest.

3. Knead gently until the mixture forms a smooth dough, then form into cylinder 6 cm in diameter and roll in granulated sugar.

4. Slice the roll into 1 cm thick slices and spread them out on the baking tray.

5. Bake the biscuits for 15-20 minutes, turning the tray round halfway through.

6. Transfer the biscuits to a wire rack and leave to cool.

Quinoa biscuits

MAKES: 35 | PREP TIME: 40 MINUTES | COOKING TIME: 20-25 MINUTES

INGREDIENTS

150 g / 5 ½ oz / 1 ½ cup quinoa flakes

50 g / 1 ¾ oz / ½ cup porridge oats

125 g / 4 ½ oz / ¾ cup stoneground wholemeal flour

1 tsp baking powder

175 g / 6 oz / ¾ cup butter

150 g / 5 ½ oz / ¾ cup soft brown sugar

110 g / 4 oz / ½ cup raw quinoa

METHOD

1. Put the quinoa flakes, oats, flour and baking powder in a food processor and blitz until fine.

2. Cream the butter with the sugar then beat in the dry ingredients.

3. Bring the dough together and shape into a log then chill for 30 minutes.

4. Preheat the oven to 180°C (160°C fan) / 350F / gas 4. Line 2 baking sheets with greaseproof paper.

5. Slice the log into 1 cm slices and roll in the raw quinoa to coat.

6. Transfer the biscuits to the prepared trays and bake for 20–25 minutes or until cooked through and golden brown.

7. Transfer the biscuits to a wire rack and leave to cool completely.

Rich chocolate tart

SERVES: 8 | PREP TIME: 3 HOURS | COOKING TIME: 15-20 MINUTES

INGREDIENTS

250 ml / 9 fl. oz / 1 cup double (heavy) cream

250 g / 9 oz dark chocolate (minimum 60 % cocoa solids), chopped

55 g / 2 oz / ¼ cup butter, softened

FOR THE PASTRY:

100 g / 3 ½ oz / ½ cup butter, cubed

200 g / 7 oz / 1 ⅓ cup plain (all-purpose) flour

55 g / 2 oz / ¼ cup caster (superfine) sugar

1 egg, beaten

METHOD

1. Preheat the oven to 200°C (180°C fan) / 400F / gas 6.

2. To make the pastry, rub the butter into the flour and sugar. Add the egg, with a little water to bind.

3. Wrap the dough in cling film. Chill for 30 minutes then roll out on a floured surface.

4. Use the pastry to line a 23 cm loose-bottomed tart tin. Trim the edges. Prick the pastry with a fork, line with baking paper and fill with baking beans.

5. Bake for 10 minutes then remove the paper and baking beans. Cook for 8 minutes until crisp.

6. Heat the cream to simmering point then pour it over the chocolate and stir until smooth. Add the butter and blend it in with a stick blender.

7. Pour the ganache into the pastry case and level the top with a palette knife. Leave the ganache to cool and set for 2 hours before cutting and serving.

Ginger snap biscuits

MAKES: 36 | PREP TIME: 15 MINUTES | COOKING TIME: 12-15 MINUTES

INGREDIENTS

75 g / 2 ½ oz / ⅓ cup butter, softened

100 g / 3 ½ oz / ⅓ cup golden syrup

225 g / 8 oz / 1 ½ cups self-raising flour

100 g / 3 ½ oz / ½ cup caster (superfine) sugar

1 tsp ground ginger

1 large egg, beaten

METHOD

1. Preheat the oven to 180°C (160°C fan) / 350F / gas 4 and line 2 baking sheets with greaseproof paper.

2. Melt the butter and golden syrup together in a saucepan.

3. Mix the flour, sugar and ground ginger together then stir in the melted butter mixture and the beaten egg.

4. Use a teaspoon to portion the mixture onto the baking trays, leaving plenty of room for the biscuits to spread.

5. Bake in batches for 12-15 minutes or until golden brown.

6. Transfer the biscuits to a wire rack and leave to cool and harden.

Almond and white chocolate blondies

MAKES: 9 | PREP TIME: 25 MINUTES | COOKING TIME: 35-40 MINUTES

INGREDIENTS

110 g / 4 oz white chocolate, chopped

225 g / 8 oz / 1 cup butter

450 g / 15 oz / 2 ½ cups light brown sugar

4 large eggs

110 g / 4 oz / ⅔ cup self-raising flour

110 g / 4 oz / ⅔ cup almonds

METHOD

1. Preheat the oven to 170°C (150°C fan) / 340F / gas 3 and oil and line a 20 x 20 cm cake tin.

2. Melt the chocolate and butter together in a saucepan, then leave to cool a little.

3. Whisk the sugar and eggs together with an electric whisk for 3 minutes or until very light and creamy.

4. Pour in the chocolate mixture and sieve over the flour, then fold everything together with the almonds until evenly mixed.

5. Scrape into the tin and bake for 35-40 minutes or until the outside is set, but the centre is still quite soft, as it will continue to cook as it cools.

6. Leave the blondie to cool completely before cutting into 9 squares.

Lemon meringue pie

SERVES: 8 | PREP TIME: 55 MINUTES | COOKING TIME: 25-30 MINUTES

INGREDIENTS

FOR THE FILLING:

2 tsp cornflour (cornstarch)

4 lemons, zest and juice

4 large eggs, beaten

225 g / 8 oz / 1 cup butter

175 g / 6 oz / ¾ cups caster
(superfine) sugar

FOR THE PASTRY:

100 g / 3 ½ oz / ½ cups butter, cubed

200 g / 7 oz / 1 ⅓ cups plain (all-purpose) flour

FOR THE MERINGUE:

4 large egg whites

110g / 4 oz / ½ cups caster
(superfine) sugar

METHOD

1. Preheat the oven to 200°C (180°C fan)
    / 400F / gas 6.

2. Make the pastry by rubbing the butter into
    the flour and adding just enough cold water
    to bind. Chill for 30 minutes then roll out on
    a floured surface.

3. Use the pastry to line a 24 cm loose-
    bottomed tart tin and prick it with a fork.

4. Line the pastry with baking paper
    and fill with baking beans or rice, then bake
    for 10 minutes. Remove the baking paper
    and beans and cook for 8 minutes until crisp.

5. Meanwhile, dissolve the cornflour in the
    lemon juice and put it in a saucepan with the
    rest of the filling ingredients.

6. Stir constantly over a medium heat to melt
    the butter and dissolve the sugar. Bring to a
    simmer then pour it into the pastry case.

7. Whisk the egg whites until stiff, then add the
    sugar and whisk until the mixture is shiny.

8. Spoon the meringue on top of the lemon
    curd, making peaks with the spoon.

9. Bake for 10 minutes or until golden brown.

Grape clafoutis

SERVES: 6 | PREP TIME: 15 MINUTES | COOKING TIME: 35 MINUTES

INGREDIENTS

75 g / 2 ½ oz / ⅓ cup butter

75 g / 2 ½ oz / ⅓ cup caster (superfine) sugar

300 ml / 10 ½ fl. oz / 1 ¼ cups whole milk

2 large eggs

50 g / 1 ¾ oz / ⅓ cup plain (all-purpose) flour

2 tbsp ground almonds

1 lemon, zest finely grated

300 g / 10 ½ oz / 2 cups mixed seedless grapes

METHOD

1. Preheat the oven to 190°C (170°C fan) / 375F / gas 5.

2. Melt the butter in a pan. Brush some of the melted butter around the inside of a 20 cm round pie dish. Add a spoonful of caster sugar. Shake to coat.

3. Whisk together the milk and eggs with the rest of the butter. Sift the flour into a separate bowl. Stir in the ground almonds, lemon zest and the rest of the sugar.

4. Make a well in the middle of the dry ingredients. Whisk in the liquid until it is a smooth batter.

5. Arrange the grapes in the prepared pie dish. Pour over the batter. Transfer to the oven.

6. Bake the clafoutis for 35 minutes. Serve warm or at room temperature.

Plum tartlets

MAKES: 6 | PREP TIME: 15 MINUTES | COOKING TIME: 25-35 MINUTES

INGREDIENTS

110 g / 4 oz / ½ cup butter, cubed and chilled

110 g / 4 oz / ⅔ cup plain (all-purpose) flour

110 g / 4 oz / ⅔ cup stoneground wholemeal flour

450 g / 1 lb plums, halved and stoned

450 g / 1 lb / 1 ¼ cup plum jam (jelly)

METHOD

1. Preheat the oven to 200°C (180°C fan) / 400F / gas 6.

2. Rub the butter into the flours until the mixture resembles fine breadcrumbs.

3. Stir in just enough cold water to bring the pastry together into a pliable dough.

4. Roll out the pastry on a floured surface and cut out 6 circles then use them to line 6 tartlet tins.

5. Arrange the halved plums in the pastry case and spoon over the jam.

6. Bake for 25-35 minutes or until the pastry is crisp and the jam has melted.

Wholemeal berry tart

SERVES: 8 | PREP TIME: 50 MINUTES | COOKING TIME: 45-55 MINUTES

INGREDIENTS

200 g / 7 oz raspberries

FOR THE PASTRY:
100 g / 3 ½ oz / cup butter, cubed
200 g / 7 oz / 1 ⅓ cups stoneground wholemeal flour

FOR THE CUSTARD:
4 large egg yolks
75 g / 2 ½ oz / ⅓ cup caster (superfine) sugar
1 tsp vanilla extract
2 tsp cornflour (cornstarch)
450 ml / 16 fl. oz / 1 cups whole milk

METHOD

1. Preheat the oven to 200°C (180°C fan) / 400F / gas 6.

2. Rub the butter into the flour and add just enough cold water to bind. Chill for 30 minutes. Roll out on a floured surface. Use the pastry to line a 23 cm round tart tin.

3. Prick the pastry with a fork, line with baking paper and fill with baking beans or rice. Bake for 10 minutes then remove the paper and baking beans and cook for another 8 minutes to crisp.

4. Reduce the oven temperature to 170°C (150°C fan) / 340F / gas 3.

5. Whisk together the custard ingredients and pour into the pastry case. Arrange the raspberries on top.

6. Bake the tart for 25-35 minutes.

156

Cherry chocolate pudding

SERVES: 8 | PREP TIME: 6 HOURS 30 MINUTES

INGREDIENTS

300 g / 10 ½ oz cherries, stoned and halved

4 tbsp caster (superfine) sugar

1 tbsp kirsch

6 slices white bread, crusts removed

250 ml / 9 fl. oz / 1 cup double (heavy) cream

250 g / 9 oz dark chocolate (min. 60% cocoa solids), chopped

METHOD

1. Put the cherries in a bowl with the sugar and kirsch and leave to macerate for 2 hours. Line a pudding basin with cling film.

2. Put the cherries in a sieve and collect the juice. Dip the bread in the cherry juice and use it to line the pudding basin. Save one slice for the lid.

3. Bring the cream to a simmer then pour it over the chocolate and stir gently to emulsify. Fold the cherries into the chocolate ganache and spoon it into the pudding basin.

4. Top with the last slice of soaked bread then cover the basin with cling film. Put a small board on top of the pudding basin and weigh it down with a can, then leave it to chill in the fridge for at least 4 hours.

5. When ready to serve, invert the pudding onto a plate and peel away the cling film.

Fresh fruit sponge pudding

SERVES: 6 | PREP TIME: 15 MINUTES | COOKING TIME: 30-35 MINUTES

INGREDIENTS

110 g / 4 oz / ⅔ cup self-raising flour, sifted

110 g / 4 oz / ½ cup caster (superfine) sugar

110 g / 4 oz / ½ cup butter, softened

2 large eggs

1 tsp vanilla extract

2 plums, cut into eighths

55 g / 1 oz / ⅓ cup raspberries

55 g / 1 oz / ⅓ cup seedless black grapes

custard or cream, to serve

METHOD

1. Preheat the oven to 190°C (170°C fan) / 375F / gas 5 and butter a small baking dish.

2. Combine the flour, sugar, butter, eggs and vanilla extract in a bowl and whisk together for 2 minutes or until smooth.

3. Arrange half of the fruit in the baking dish and spoon in the cake mixture. Top with the rest of the fruit then bake for 30-35 minutes.

4. Test with a wooden toothpick; if it comes out clean, the cake is done.

5. Serve warm with custard or cream.

Berry chocolate brownies

MAKES: 9 | PREP TIME: 25 MINUTES | COOKING TIME: 35 MINUTES

INGREDIENTS

110 g / 4 oz dark chocolate (min. 60% cocoa solids), chopped

85 g / 3 oz / ¾ cup unsweetened cocoa powder, sifted

225 g / 8 oz / 1 cup butter

450 g / 15 oz / 2 ½ cups light brown sugar

4 large eggs

110 g / 4 oz / ⅔ cup self-raising flour

175 g / 6 oz / 1 ¼ cups mixed berries

METHOD

1. Preheat the oven to 170°C (150°C fan) / 340F / gas 3 and oil and line a 20 x 20 cm cake tin.

2. Melt the chocolate, cocoa and butter together in a pan, then leave to cool a little.

3. Whisk the sugar and eggs together with an electric whisk for 3 minutes or until creamy.

4. Pour in the chocolate mixture and sieve over the flour. Reserve some of the berries for decoration. Add the rest to the bowl, then fold everything together until evenly mixed.

5. Scrape into the tin and bake for 35 minutes or until the outside is set, but the centre is still soft, as it will continue to cook as it cools.

6. Leave the brownie to cool then cut into nine squares.

159

Almond filo pie

SERVES: 8 | PREP TIME: 25 MINUTES | COOKING TIME: 35-40 MINUTES

INGREDIENTS

450 g / 1 lb filo pastry

200 g / 7 oz / ¾ cup butter, melted

450 g / 1 lb / 3 cups blanched almonds

100 g / 3 ½ oz / ½ cup caster (superfine) sugar

1 lemon, zest finely grated

icing (confectioner's) sugar to dust

METHOD

1. Preheat the oven to 180°C (160°C fan) / 350F / gas 4 and butter a round baking dish.

2. Brush 10 sheets of filo pastry with melted butter and use to line the baking dish.

3. Put the almonds, sugar and lemon zest in a food processor and pulse until finely chopped Add half of the remaining butter. Pulse again.

4. Spread a third of the almond mixture across the bottom of the pastry case. Top with a third of the remaining pastry sheets, making sure each one is well buttered.

5. Continue layering, finishing with a layer of buttered filo, then fold in the edges to neaten.

6. Bake the pie in the oven for 35-45 minutes or until the pastry is golden and cooked through.

7. Unmould the pie and dust with icing sugar.

Cherry clafoutis

MAKES: 6 | PREP TIME: 45 MINUTES | COOKING TIME: 40 MINUTES

INGREDIENTS

300 g / 10 ½ oz cherries, stoned

2 tbsp kirsch

75 g / 2 ½ oz / ⅓ cup butter

75 g / 2 ½ oz / ⅓ cup caster (superfine) sugar

300 ml / 10 ½ fl. oz / 1 ¼ cups whole milk

2 large eggs

50 g / 1 ¾ oz / ⅓ cup plain (all-purpose) flour

2 tbsp ground almonds

METHOD

1. Preheat the oven to 190°C (170°C fan) / 375F / gas 5. Put the cherries in a bowl with the kirsch and leave to marinate for 30 minutes.

2. Melt the butter in a pan. Brush it around the inside of a 20 cm quiche dish. Add a spoonful of caster sugar. Shake to coat.

3. Whisk together the milk and eggs with the rest of the butter.

4. Sift the flour into a mixing bowl with a pinch of salt and stir in the ground almonds and the rest of the sugar. Make a well in the middle of the dry ingredients and whisk in the liquid until you have a lump-free batter.

5. Arrange the cherries in the prepared baking dish, pour over the batter and transfer to the oven.

6. Bake the clafoutis for 40 minutes or until a skewer inserted in the centre comes out clean. Serve.

Chocolate berry tartlets

MAKES: 10 | PREP TIME: 1 HOUR | COOKING TIME: 10 MINUTES

INGREDIENTS

120 g / 4 ¼ oz / ¾ cup plain (all-purpose) flour

120 g / 4 ¼ oz / ¾ cup ground almonds

100 g / 3 ½ oz / ½ cup golden caster (superfine) sugar

a pinch of salt

100 g / 3 ½ oz / ½ cup unsalted butter, cut into cubes

2 large egg yolks

250 g / 9 oz white chocolate

200 ml / 7 fl. oz / ¾ cup double (heavy) cream

1 vanilla pod, cut in half and seeds scraped out

200 g / 7 oz / 1 ⅓ cups mixed berries and fruit, chopped

50 g / 1 ¾ oz / ⅔ cup flaked (slivered) almonds

mint sprigs and icing (confectioner's) sugar

METHOD

1. Put the flour, ground almonds, sugar and salt in a blender. Blend briefly to combine. Add the butter. Pulse until the mixture resembles breadcrumbs.

2. Turn out into a bowl. Add the egg yolks. Mix with a knife to form a coarse breadcrumb mixture.

3. Turn out onto a floured surface and combine into a smooth dough. Roll into a ball and wrap in cling film. Refrigerate to chill for at least 30 minutes.

4. Preheat the oven to 180°C (160°C fan) / 350F / gas 4 and lightly grease a muffin tin.

5. Roll out the dough to around 3mm thick. Cut out into rounds and press into the muffin tin, the sides should be above the level of the tin. Prick the bottom with a fork and line with greaseproof paper and weigh down with baking beans. Bake for 10 minute until golden, removing the lining and baking beans midway through. Remove to cool, loosening them in the tin to ensure that they can be removed.

6. Break the chocolate into a heatproof bowl. Gently heat the cream and vanilla pod and seeds in a saucepan until just about simmering. Remove the vanilla pod and pour over the chocolate while gently mixing to melt and form a thick ganache. Allow to cool slightly before pouring into the tartlets. Place in the refrigerator to set.

7. To serve, top the tarts with the chopped fresh fruit and berries and garnish with mint sprigs and a dusting of icing sugar.

Brioche cream buns

MAKES: 12 | PREP TIME: 4 HOURS 30 MINUTES | COOKING TIME: 10-15 MINUTES

INGREDIENTS

250 g / 9 oz / 1 ¼ cups butter, cubed

400 g / 14 oz / 2 ⅔ cups strong white bread flour

2 ½ tsp easy blend dried yeast

4 tbsp caster (superfine) sugar

1 tsp fine sea salt

4 large eggs, plus 3 extra yolks

TO FINISH

1 egg, beaten

4 tbsp sugar nibs

300 ml / 10 ½ fl. oz / 1 ¼ cups whipped cream

METHOD

1. Rub the butter into the flour then stir in the yeast, sugar and salt. Beat the whole eggs and yolks together and stir into the dry ingredients.

2. Knead the dough on a lightly oiled surface with 2 plastic scrapers for 10 minutes until smooth.

3. Leave the dough to rest in a lightly oiled bowl, covered with oiled cling film, for 2 hours.

4. Divide the dough into 12 balls and transfer them to a greased baking tray.

5. Cover with oiled cling film and leave to prove for 2 hours or until doubled in size.

6. Meanwhile, preheat the oven to 220°C (200°C fan) / 425F / gas 7. Once risen, brush the tops with beaten egg and sprinkle with sugar nibs then bake for 10-15 minutes.

7. Transfer the rolls to a wire rack and leave to cool completely before splitting and filling with whipped cream.

Biscuit brownies

MAKES: 9 | PREP TIME: 25 MINUTES | COOKING TIME: 35 MINUTES

INGREDIENTS

110 g / 4 oz milk chocolate, chopped

85 g / 3 oz / ¾ cup cocoa powder, sifted

225 g / 8 oz / 1 cup butter

450 g / 15 oz / 2 ½ cups light brown sugar

4 large eggs

110 g / 4 oz / ⅔ cup self-raising flour

8 sponge finger biscuits, broken
into pieces

METHOD

1. Preheat the oven to 170°C (150°C fan) / 340F / gas 3 and oil and line a 20 x 20 cm cake tin.

2. Melt the chocolate, cocoa and butter together in a saucepan, then leave to cool.

3. Whisk the sugar and eggs together with an electric whisk for 3 minutes or until creamy.

4. Pour in the chocolate mixture and sieve over the flour, then fold everything together with the sponge finger biscuits until mixed.

5. Scrape into the tin and bake for 35 minutes or until a skewer inserted comes out clean.

6. Leave the brownie to cool completely before cutting into nine squares.

Baked cheesecake

MAKES: 8 | PREP TIME: 30 MINUTES | COOKING TIME: 50 MINUTES

INGREDIENTS

250 g / 9 oz digestive biscuits

150 g / 5 ¼ oz / ⅔ cup unsalted butter, melted

300 g / 10 ½ oz / 1 ⅓ cups caster (superfine) sugar

175 g / 6 oz dark chocolate

500 g / 1 lb 1 oz cream cheese

150 ml / 5 ¼ fl. oz / ⅔ cup double (heavy) cream

1 tsp vanilla extract

4 eggs

METHOD

1. Preheat the oven to 160°C (140°C fan) / 325F / gas 3.

2. Place the biscuits into a bag. Crush them using a rolling pin. Mix them with the melted butter and 50 g sugar. Press into a 20 cm spring-form cake tin.

3. Melt the chocolate in a bain-marie. Leave to cool.

4. Whisk the remaining sugar with the cream cheese, cream, vanilla and eggs. Mix two-thirds of the cream cheese mixture into the melted chocolate so that you have two different fillings. Pour the chocolate filling into the prepared cake tin before adding the vanilla in rings.

5. Bake in the oven for around 50 minutes until the filling is set. Remove and allow to cool fully before serving.

Lemon madeleines

MAKES: 12 | PREP TIME: 1 HOUR 30 MINUTES | COOKING TIME: 10-15 MINUTES

INGREDIENTS

110 g / 4 oz / ½ cup butter

55 g / 2 oz / ⅓ cup plain (all-purpose) flour

1 lemon, zest finely grated

55 g / 2 oz / ½ cup ground almonds

110 g / 4 oz / 1 cup icing (confectioner's) sugar

3 large egg whites

METHOD

1. Heat the butter until it foams then leave to cool.

2. Combine the flour, lemon zest, ground almonds and the icing sugar in a bowl and whisk in the egg whites.

3. Pour the cooled butter into the bowl and whisk into the mixture until evenly mixed.

4. Leave the cake mixture in the fridge for 1 hour.

5. Preheat the oven to 170°C (150°C fan) / 325F / gas 3 and oil and flour a 12-hole madeleine mould.

6. Spoon the mixture into the moulds then transfer the tin to the oven and bake for 10-15 minutes.

7. Test with a wooden toothpick. If it comes out clean, the cakes are done. Transfer the cakes to a wire rack to cool for 5 minutes before serving.

Strawberry custard tartlets

MAKES: 6 | PREP TIME: 45 MINUTES | COOKING TIME: 15-20 MINUTES

INGREDIENTS

200 g / 7 oz strawberries, sliced

FOR THE PASTRY:

200 g / 7 oz / 1 ⅓ cups plain (all-purpose) flour

100 g / 3 ½ oz / ½ cup butter, cubed

FOR THE CUSTARD:

2 large egg yolks

55 g / 2 oz / ¼ cup caster (superfine) sugar

1 tsp vanilla extract

2 tsp cornflour (cornstarch)

225 ml / 8 fl. oz / ¾ cup whole milk

METHOD

1. To make the pastry, rub the butter into the flour. Add a little water to bind. Chill for 30 minutes.

2. Preheat the oven to 200°C (180°C fan) / 400F / gas 6.

3. Roll out the pastry on a floured surface. Use it to line 6 tartlet cases.

4. Arrange the strawberry slices in the pastry cases.

5. Whisk the custard ingredients together in a jug and three-quarters fill the pastry cases.

6. Bake the tarts for 15-20 minutes or until the custard has set and the pastry is crisp.

169

Wholemeal oat cookies

MAKES: 35 | PREP TIME: 15 MINUTES | COOKING TIME: 12-15 MINUTES

INGREDIENTS

175 g / 6 oz / ¾ cup butter, melted

225 g / 8 oz / 1 ⅓ cup dark brown sugar

100 g / 3 ½ oz / ½ cup caster (superfine) sugar

2 tsp vanilla extract

1 egg, plus 1 egg yolk

125 g / 4 ½ oz / ¾ cup self-raising flour

125 g / 4 ½ oz / ¾ cup stoneground wholemeal flour

125 g / 4 ½ oz / 1 ¼ cup oats

METHOD

1. Preheat the oven to 170°C (150°C fan) / 340F / gas 3 and line two baking sheets with greaseproof paper.

2. Cream together the butter, two sugars and vanilla extract until pale and well whipped, then beat in the egg and yolk, followed by the flours and oats.

3. Drop tablespoons of the mixture onto the prepared trays, leaving plenty of room to spread.

4. Bake the cookies in batches for 12-15 minutes or until the edges are starting to brown, but the centres are still chewy.

5. Transfer to a wire rack and leave to cool.

Orange custard tartlets

MAKES: 6 | PREP TIME: 45 MINUTES | COOKING TIME: 25-30 MINUTES

INGREDIENTS

FOR THE PASTRY:

200 g / 7 oz / 1 ⅓ cups plain (all-purpose) flour

100 g / 3 ½ oz / ½ cup butter, cubed

FOR THE CUSTARD:

2 large egg yolks

55 g / 2 oz / ¼ cup caster (superfine) sugar

2 tsp cornflour (cornstarch)

125 ml / 4 ½ fl. oz / ½ cup whole milk

100 ml / 3 ½ fl. oz / ½ cup fresh orange juice, sieved

1 tbsp orange zest, finely grated

METHOD

1. To make the pastry, rub the butter into the flour. Add a little water to bind. Chill for 30 minutes.

2. Preheat the oven to 200°C (180°C fan) / 400F / gas 6.

3. Roll out the pastry on a floured surface and use it to line 6 tartlet cases.

4. Prick the pastry with a fork, line with baking paper and fill with baking beans or rice.

5. Bake for 10 minutes then remove the paper and baking beans.

6. Whisk the custard ingredients together in a jug and three-quarters fill the pastry cases.

7. Bake the tarts for 15-20 minutes or until the custard has set and the pastry is crisp.

Chocolate brownies

MAKES: 9 | PREP TIME: 20 MINUTES | COOKING TIME: 35-40 MINUTES

INGREDIENTS

110 g / 4 oz milk chocolate, chopped

85 g / 3 oz / ¾ cup unsweetened cocoa powder, sifted

225 g / 8 oz / 1 cup butter

450 g /15 oz / 2 ½ cups light brown sugar

4 large eggs

110 g / 4 oz / ⅔ cup self-raising flour

METHOD

1. Preheat the oven to 170°C (150°C fan) / 340F / gas 3. Oil and line a 20 x 20 cm cake tin.

2. Melt the chocolate, cocoa and butter together in a saucepan, then leave to cool a little.

3. Whisk the sugar and eggs together with an electric whisk for 3 minutes until very creamy.

4. Pour in the chocolate mixture. Sieve over the flour. Fold everything together until mixed.

5. Scrape into the tin and bake for 35-40 minutes or until the outside is set, but the centre is still quite soft, as it will continue to cook as it cools.

6. Leave the brownie to cool completely before cutting into 9 squares.

172

Chocolate, orange and almond torte

SERVES: 6 | PREP TIME: 25 MINUTES | COOKING TIME: 30 MINUTES

INGREDIENTS

2 large eggs, separated

150 g / 5 ½ oz / ⅔ cup caster (superfine) sugar

75 g / 2 ½ oz / ⅓ cup butter

2 tbsp unsweetened cocoa powder

100 g / 3 ½ oz dark chocolate (min. 60%
cocoa solids), chopped

150 g / 5 ½ oz / 1 ½ cups ground almonds

1 orange, zest finely grated

TO DECORATE:

100 g / 3 ½ oz / ½ cup caster (superfine) sugar

6 almonds

1 orange, zest finely pared

METHOD

1. Preheat the oven to 180°C (160°C fan) / 350F /
gas 4 and line a round spring-form cake tin.

2. Whisk the egg yolks and sugar together for
4 minutes. Melt the butter, cocoa and chocolate,
then fold into the egg yolk mixture with the
ground almonds.

3. Whip the egg whites to stiff peaks and fold them
into the cake mixture. Scrape the mixture into the
tin and bake for 30 minutes or until just set.
Transfer to a wire rack to cool.

4. Heat the sugar in a pan until it has turned a light
caramel colour. Use a fork to dip the almonds and
orange zest in the caramel. Leave to set on a baking
mat. Cut the torte into wedges and decorate with
the caramel almonds and orange zest.

Summer berry tartlets

MAKES: 6 | PREP TIME: 45 MINUTES | COOKING TIME: 18 MINUTES

INGREDIENTS

450 g / 1 lb / 2 cups mascarpone

100 g / 3 ½ oz / 1 cup icing (confectioner's) sugar

1 tsp vanilla extract

12 strawberries, halved

12 raspberries

100 g / 3 ½ oz blueberries

6 sprigs redcurrants

FOR THE PASTRY:

100 g / 3 ½ oz / ½ cup butter, cubed

200 g / 7 oz / 1 ⅓ cups plain (all-purpose) flour

1 egg, beaten

METHOD

1. Preheat the oven to 200°C (180°C fan) / 400F / gas 6.

2. To make the pastry, rub the butter into the flour and add just enough cold water to bind.

3. Chill for 30 minutes then roll out on a floured surface. Use the pastry to line 6 tartlet cases.

4. Prick the pastry with a fork, line with baking paper and fill with baking beans. Bake for 10 minutes then remove the paper and beans.

5. Brush the inside of the pastry cases with beaten egg. Cook for 8 minutes until crisp.

6. Whisk the mascarpone with the icing sugar and vanilla extract until smooth.

7. When the pastry cases have cooled to room temperature, spoon in the filling. Level the tops.

8. Arrange the fruit on top of the filling and serve.

One-Crust Apple Pie

SERVES: 6 | PREP TIME: 25 MINUTES | COOKING TIME: 40 MINUTES

INGREDIENTS

1 large bramley apple, peeled, cored and chopped

1 tsp ground cinnamon

1 tsp cornflour (cornstarch)

3 tbsp caster (superfine) sugar

3 eating apples, peeled, cored and sliced

100 ml / 3 ½ fl. oz / ½ cup apricot jam (jelly)

FOR THE PASTRY:

150 g / 5 ½ oz / ⅔ cup butter, cubed and chilled

300 g / 10 ½ oz / 2 cups plain (all purpose) flour

METHOD

1. Preheat the oven to 200°C (180°C fan) / 400F / gas 6.

2. To make the pastry, rub the butter into the flour then add just enough cold water to form a pliable dough. Roll out the pastry into a large circle and transfer it to a baking tray.

3. Toss the chopped bramley with the cinnamon, cornflour and sugar, then pile it into the centre of the pastry, leaving an 8 cm (3 in) border round the outside. Top with the sliced apples, then fold the outside edge of the pastry up and over the top, crimping to hold it in place where necessary.

4. Bake the pie for 40 minutes or until the pastry is cooked through underneath. Heat the jam in a small saucepan, then spoon it over the top of the apples. Serve hot or cold.

Red velvet cheesecake

MAKES: 8 | PREP TIME: 30 MINUTES | COOKING TIME: 30 MINUTES

INGREDIENTS

120 g / 4 ¼ oz / ½ cup unsalted butter

250 g / 9 oz / 1 ¼ cups caster (superfine) sugar

1 tbsp red food colouring

3 large eggs, beaten

50 g / 1 ¾ oz / ¼ cup cocoa powder

120 g / 4 ¼ oz / ¾ cup plain (all-purpose) flour

250 g / 9 oz / 2 ½ cups cream cheese

METHOD

1. Preheat the oven to 180°C (160°C fan) / 350F / gas 4. Grease and line a 20cm square baking tray.

2. Cream together the butter and 200 g sugar. Add the food colouring, 2 teaspoons of the eggs, the cocoa and flour and mix until a batter forms.

3. In a separate bowl, whisk the cream cheese. Add the remaining sugar and egg. Continue to whisk until any lumps have disappeared.

4. In the baking tray, add layers of the red velvet mix followed by the cream cheese finishing with a layer of cream cheese. Use a spatula to smooth out each layer before adding the next.

5. Bake in the oven for 30 minutes until a skewer inserted into the centre comes out clean. Remove and allow to cool then cut into rectangles. Dust with cocoa to serve as desired.

Baked ring doughnuts

MAKES: 8 | PREP TIME: 20 MINUTES | COOKING TIME: 10-15 MINUTES

INGREDIENTS

125 g / 4 ¼ oz / ¾ cup plain (all-purpose) flour

1 tsp baking powder

1 tsp bicarbonate of (baking) soda

1 large free-range egg

70 g / 2 ½ oz / ⅓ cup caster (superfine) sugar

50 ml / 1 ¾ fl. oz / ¼ cup milk

50 g / 1 ¾ oz / ¼ cup buttermilk

30 g unsalted butter, melted

1 orange, zest only

100 g / 3 ½ oz / 1 cup icing (confectioner's) sugar

METHOD

1. Preheat the oven to 180°C (160°C fan) / 350F / gas 4 and lightly grease a doughnut pan.

2. Combine the flour, baking powder and bicarbonate of soda in a large mixing bowl.

3. In a separate bowl, whisk together the egg, sugar, milk, buttermilk and butter.

4. Pour the wet ingredients into the dry. Mix to combine then stir through the orange zest. The batter should be fairly thick.

5. Spoon the batter into the doughnut moulds and place into the oven to bake for 10-15 minutes until golden. Remove from the oven and turn out onto a wire rack to cool.

6. Dust with the icing sugar before serving.

177

Iced ring doughnuts

MAKES: 8 | PREP TIME: 25 MINUTES | COOKING TIME: 10-15 MINUTES

INGREDIENTS

125 g / 4 ¼ oz / ¾ cup plain (all-purpose) flour

1 tsp baking powder

½ tsp bicarbonate of (baking) soda

1 tsp cinnamon

1 large free-range egg

70 g / 2 ½ oz / ⅓ cup caster (superfine) sugar

50 ml / 1 ¾ fl. oz / ¼ cup milk

50 g / 1 ¾ oz / ¼ cup buttermilk

30 g / 1 oz unsalted butter, melted

FOR THE TOPPING:

150 g / 5 ¼ oz dark chocolate

100 ml / 3 ½ fl. oz / ½ cup double (heavy) cream

50 g / 1 ¾ oz / ½ cup icing (confectioner's) sugar

100 g / 3 ½ oz assorted chocolate sprinkles

METHOD

1. Preheat the oven to 180°C (160°C fan) / 350F / gas 4 and lightly grease a doughnut pan.

2. Combine the flour, baking powder, bicarbonate of soda and cinnamon in a large mixing bowl.

3. In a separate bowl, whisk together the egg, sugar, milk, buttermilk and butter.

4. Pour the wet ingredients into the dry and mix to combine. The batter will be fairly thick, so take care not to over mix.

5. Spoon the batter into the doughnut moulds and place into the oven to bake for 10-15 minutes until golden. Remove from the oven and turn out onto a wire rack to cool.

6. To make the topping, break the chocolate into chunks and place into a bowl. Heat the cream to a low simmer. Pour over the chocolate and mix to melt the chocolate, adding the icing sugar and mixing until any lumps disappear.

7. Gently dunk the cooled doughnuts into the topping mixture before adding the sprinkles.

Teacakes

MAKES: 8 | PREP TIME: 20 MINUTES | COOKING TIME: 15 MINUTES

INGREDIENTS

75 g / 2 ½ oz / ½ cup wholemeal flour

75 g / 2 ½ oz / ½ cup plain (all-purpose) flour

a pinch of salt

200 g / 7 oz / ¾ cup caster (superfine) sugar

½ tsp baking powder

50 g / 1 ¾ oz / ¼ cup unsalted butter

2 tbsp milk

3 free-range egg whites

75 g / 2 ½ oz chocolate sprinkles

METHOD

1. Preheat the oven to 160°C (140°C fan) / 325F / gas 3 and line a baking tray with greaseproof paper.

2. Add the first five ingredients to a bowl. Rub in the butter until the mixture resembles breadcrumbs. Add the milk and mix until a dough forms.

3. Roll the dough out to 2 cm thickness. Cut out eight rounds with a cutter. Place onto the prepared tray. Chill for 10 minutes in the fridge.

4. Bake in the oven for 15 minutes. Remove from the oven. Place onto a wire rack to cool.

5. Place the remaining sugar onto a baking tray. Spread evenly. Place into the warm oven for 5 minutes to warm but not colour.

6. Whisk the egg whites until soft peaks form. Gradually add the warmed sugar until the mixture becomes stiff and silky.

7. Spoon the meringue onto the biscuits into a dome shape. Cover with the chocolate sprinkles.

Pear and almond tart

SERVES: 8 | PREP TIME: 25 MINUTES | COOKING TIME: 25 MINUTES

INGREDIENTS

150 g / 5 ½ oz / 1 ½ cups ground almonds

150 g / 5 ½ oz / ⅔ cup butter, softened

150 g / 5 ½ oz / ⅔ cup caster (superfine) sugar

2 large eggs

2 tbsp plain (all-purpose) flour

1 pastry case

4 pears, cored and quartered

4 tbsp apricot jam (jelly)

2 tbsp flaked (slivered) almonds

METHOD

1. Preheat the oven to 200°C (180°C fan) / 400F / gas 6.

2. Whisk together the almonds, butter, sugar, eggs and flour until smoothly whipped and spoon the mixture into the pastry case.

3. Press the pear quarters into the frangipane and bake the tart for 25 minutes or until the frangipane is cooked through.

4. Heat the apricot jam until runny and brush it over the pears then sprinkle with flaked almonds.

Candied fruit loaf

SERVES: 8 | PREP TIME: 20 MINUTES | COOKING TIME: 45 MINUTES

INGREDIENTS

225 g / 8 oz / 1 ½ cups self-raising flour

110 g / 3 ¾ oz / ½ cup unsalted butter

110 g / 3 ¾ oz / ½ cup caster (superfine) sugar

120 g / 4 ¼ oz / 1 cup candied fruit

1 lemon, zest only

1 egg, beaten

75 ml / 2 ½ fl. oz / ⅓ cup milk

1 tsp vanilla extract

METHOD

1. Preheat the oven to 200°C (180°C fan) / 400F / gas 6 and line a loaf tin with greaseproof paper.

2. Place the flour, butter and sugar into a blender and blend until you achieve a breadcrumb like consistency. Pour into a mixing bowl and add the candied fruit and lemon zest.

3. Combine the egg, milk and vanilla extract in a jug and whisk. Pour into the mixing bowl and stir with a wooden spoon until you have a smooth batter.

4. Pour into the prepared tin and bake in the oven for approximately 45 minutes or until a skewer inserted into the centre comes out clean. Remove to cool completely before serving.

Almond cookies

MAKES: 20 | PREP TIME: 15 MINUTES | COOKING TIME: 20 MINUTES

INGREDIENTS

150 g / 5 ¼ oz / 1 cup plain (all-purpose) flour

50 g / 1 ¾ oz / ½ cup ground almonds

50 g / 1 ¾ oz / ¼ cup caster (superfine) sugar

a pinch of salt

1 tsp vanilla extract

1 tsp almond extract

2 eggs, beaten

50 g / 1 ¾ oz / ¼ cup unsalted butter, softened

METHOD

1. Preheat the oven to 180°C (160°C fan) / 350F / gas 4 and line two baking trays with greaseproof paper.

2. Combine the flour, ground almonds, sugar and salt in a mixing bowl.

3. Mix the vanilla, almond extract and eggs in a separate bowl or jug.

4. Pour the wet ingredients into the dry and mix to combine. Add the butter to the mixture and continue to mix through.

5. Spoon the mixture onto a baking tray and bake in the oven for 20 minutes until golden. Remove from the oven to cool completely.

Churros

MAKES: 10 | PREP TIME: 40 MINUTES | COOKING TIME: 20 MINUTES

INGREDIENTS

175 ml / 6 fl. oz / ⅔ cup water

100 g / 3 ½ oz / ½ cup unsalted butter

25 g light brown sugar

a pinch of salt

100 g / 3 ½ oz / ⅔ cup plain (all-purpose) flour

2 eggs, beaten

1 tsp vanilla extract

FOR THE DIPPING SAUCE:

100 g / 3 ½ oz chocolate

150 ml / 5 ¼ fl. oz / ⅔ cup double (heavy) cream

1 vanilla pod

METHOD

1. Preheat the oven to 200°C (180°C fan) / 400F / gas 6 and line two baking trays with greaseproof paper.

2. Place the water, butter, sugar and salt into a saucepan and gently heat. Once the butter has melted and the water is coming to a simmer, remove from the heat and beat in the flour.

3. Return to the heat and continue to beat with a spoon until a dough forms. Place into a clean bowl. Set aside to cool enough to be handled.

4. Beat the eggs together with the vanilla extract. Add the eggs to the dough, mixing after each addition.

5. Pipe the mixture onto the prepared baking trays using the star nozzle. Leave enough space between them to account for some spreading. Bake in the oven for around 15-18 minutes until crisp and hollow sounding. Remove to cool.

6. Break the chocolate into a bowl. Add the cream to a saucepan and cut the vanilla pod in half, remove the seeds and add the seeds and pod to the cream. Heat gently until just about simmering, then remove the vanilla pod and pour the cream over the chocolate, whisking until a sauce forms.

7. Serve the churros with the chocolate sauce for dipping.

185

Lemon and blueberry tarts

MAKES: 12 | PREP TIME: 1 HOUR | COOKING TIME: 20 MINUTES

INGREDIENTS

175 g / 6 oz / 1 ¼ cups plain (all-purpose) flour

100 g / 3 ½ oz / ½ cup unsalted butter, cold and cut into cubes

30 g / 1 oz / ¼ cup icing (confectioner's) sugar

5 free-range eggs

175 ml / 6 fl. oz / ⅔ cup double (heavy) cream

150 g / 5 ¼ oz / ⅔ cup caster (superfine) sugar

3 lemons, juice and zest

100 g / 3 ½ oz / ⅔ cup blueberries

75 g / 2 ½ oz chocolate, broken into chunks

METHOD

1. To make the pastry, place the flour, butter and icing sugar into a food processor. Pulse until it forms a breadcrumb consistency.

2. Add one egg to the mixture and a tablespoon of cold water. Mix until a dough forms. Turn out onto a floured surface. Knead to bind the dough together, then roll into a ball, wrap in clingfilm and chill in the fridge for 15 minutes.

3. Preheat the oven to 200°C (180°C fan) / 400F / gas 6. Grease and line twelve 7.5 cm fluted tart tins.

4. Roll out the pasty to 5 mm thickness and, using a 10 cm round cutter, cut out the tart bases. Place into the tins, add a layer of baking parchment and a few baking beans.

5. Blind bake the cases for 7-8 minutes, then remove the parchment and beans and bake for a further 3-4 minutes until lightly coloured. Remove from the oven to cool and turn the heat down to 180°C (160°C fan) / 350F / gas 4.

6. In a large mixing bowl, add the remaining eggs, 100 ml cream, caster sugar and lemon. Whisk until combined, then pour into the tart bases.

7. Bake in the oven for around 7 minutes until set but slightly wobbly. Remove to cool and decorate with the fresh blueberries.

8. Heat the remaining cream in a saucepan until just about simmering, remove from the heat and stir in the chocolate chunks until smooth. Drizzle over the tarts.

Double chocolate cookies

MAKES: 12 | PREP TIME: 40 MINUTES | COOKING TIME: 12-15 MINUTES

INGREDIENTS

100 g / 3 ½ oz / ½ cup unsalted butter

100 g / 3 ½ oz / ½ cup soft brown sugar

1 large free-range egg

½ tsp vanilla extract

150 g / 5 ¼ oz / 1 cup self-raising flour

50 g / 1 ¾ oz / ¼ cup cocoa powder

100 g / 3 ½ oz plain chocolate chips

METHOD

1. Preheat the oven to 180°C (160°C fan) / 350F / gas 4 and grease and line two baking trays.

2. In a mixing bowl, cream together the butter and sugar until light and fluffy.

3. Mix the egg and vanilla extract into the butter.

4. Sift the flour and cocoa into the butter mixture and fold through before stirring in the chocolate chips.

5. Roll the dough into a thick sausage shape and wrap in cling film. Place into the refrigerator to chill for 20 minutes.

6. Remove from the refrigerator and slice into cookie shape discs, removing the cling film as you do this.

7. Place onto the prepared baking tray and bake for 12-15 minutes until golden brown and still a little chewy. Remove to cool completely.

French strawberry tarts

MAKES: 4 | PREP TIME: 1 HOUR | COOKING TIME: 20 MINUTES

INGREDIENTS

225 g / 8 oz / 1 ½ cups plain (all-purpose) flour

100 g / 3 ½ oz / ½ cup golden caster (superfine) sugar

a pinch of salt

100 g / 3 ½ oz / ½ cup unsalted butter, cold but into cubes

5 large egg yolks

275 ml / 9 ¾ fl. oz / 1 ¾ cups whole milk

1 vanilla pod, split lengthways

75 g / 2 ½ oz / ⅓ cup caster (superfine) sugar

1 tbsp cornflour (cornstarch)

1 lemon, zest only

150 g / 5 ¼ oz strawberries, sliced

METHOD

1. Add flour, golden caster sugar and salt into a blender. Blend briefly to combine. Add the butter and pulse until the mixture resembles breadcrumbs.

2. Turn out into a bowl. Add two egg yolks. Mix with a knife to form a coarse breadcrumb mixture.

3. Turn out onto a lightly floured surface. Bring together into a smooth dough, then roll into a ball. Wrap in clingfilm and refrigerate for 30 minutes.

4. Preheat the oven to 180°C (160°C fan) / 350F / gas 4 and lightly grease a four tartlet cases.

5. Roll out the dough to a 1 cm thickness. Cut out into rounds and press into the cases so that the sides are above the level of the tin. Prick the bottom with a fork and line with greaseproof paper and weigh down with baking beans. Bake for 8 minutes, removing the lining and baking beans midway through. Remove to cool.

6. While the pastry is chilling, make the crème pâtissière filling. Heat the milk and vanilla pod in a pan until just boiling. In a separate pan, whisk the remaining egg yolks and sugar until increased in volume. Beat in the cornflour and lemon zest, before straining the milk into the eggs whilst continuing to whisk.

7. Heat the mixture until thick, then cover and leave to cool.

8. Fill the cooled pastry cases with the crème pâtissière before arranging the sliced strawberries on top.

Sweet blueberry buns

MAKES: 12 | PREP TIME: 1 HOUR 45 MINUTES | COOKING TIME: 30 MINUTES

INGREDIENTS

500 g / 1 lb 1 oz / 3 ⅓ cups strong white flour

100 g / 3 ½ oz / ½ cup caster (superfine) sugar

a pinch of salt

15 g dried fast-action yeast

300 ml / 10 fl. oz / 1 ¼ cups milk

40 g / 1 ½ oz / ¼ cup unsalted butter

2 free-range eggs

200 g / 7 oz blueberry jam (jelly)

METHOD

1. Sift the flour, sugar and salt into a mixing bowl, making a well in the centre. Add the yeast.

2. Gently heat the milk and butter together until the butter has melted.

3. Pour into the dry ingredients along with one of the eggs. Gradually mix together to form a dough. Turn out onto a floured surface and knead for 5-10 minutes until smooth. Add more flour if too sticky.

4. Form into a ball and place into a lightly oiled bowl. Cover and leave somewhere warm to rise for an hour or until doubled in size.

5. Turn out the dough and gently knock back. Divide into 12 equal pieces and form into bun shapes. Place onto a lined baking tray and leave for a further 30 minutes until risen.

6. Preheat the oven to 180°C (160°C fan) / 350F / gas 4.

7. Carefully make an incision into the buns at the side and fill with the jam before sealing. Gently beat the remaining egg and brush over the top of the buns before baking in the oven for 30 minutes until golden.

Chocolate chip cookies

MAKES: 12 | PREP TIME: 40 MINUTES | COOKING TIME: 12-15 MINUTES

INGREDIENTS

100 g / 3 ½ oz / ½ cup unsalted butter

100 g / 3 ½ oz / ½ cup soft brown sugar

1 large free-range egg

½ tsp vanilla extract

200 g / 7 oz / 1 ⅓ cups self-raising flour

100 g / 3 ½ oz plain chocolate chips

METHOD

1. Preheat the oven to 180°C (160°C fan) / 350F / gas 4 and grease and line two baking trays.

2. In a large mixing bowl, cream together the butter and sugar until light and fluffy.

3. Mix the egg and vanilla extract into the butter. Sift the flour into the butter mixture and fold through before stirring in the chocolate chips.

4. Roll the dough into a thick sausage shape and wrap in cling film. Place into the refrigerator to chill for 20 minutes.

5. Remove from the refrigerator and slice into cookie shape discs, removing the cling film as you do this.

6. Place onto the prepared baking tray and bake for 12-15 minutes until golden brown and still a little chewy. Remove to cool completely.

Muffins and other bakes

Breads and savoury bakes

Wholemeal sesame baguettes

MAKES: 4 | PREP TIME: 3 HOURS 30 MINUTES | COOKING TIME: 25-30 MINUTES

INGREDIENTS

300 g / 10 ½ oz / 2 cup stoneground wholemeal flour

100 g / 3 ½ oz / ½ cup strong white bread flour, plus extra for dusting

½ tsp easy-blend dried yeast

2 tbsp caster (superfine) sugar

1 tsp fine sea salt

1 tbsp sesame oil

1 egg, beaten

3 tbsp sesame seeds

METHOD

1. Mix together the flours, yeast, sugar and salt. Stir the oil and 280ml of warm water into the dry ingredients.

2. Knead the mixture on a lightly oiled surface with your hands for 10 minutes or until smooth and elastic.

3. Leave the dough to rest in an oiled bowl, covered with oiled film, for 2 hours. Knead it for 2 more minutes then split it into 4 even pieces and shape into baguettes.

4. Transfer the baguettes to a greased baking tray and cover with oiled cling film. Leave to prove for 1 hour.

5. Preheat the oven to 220°C (200°C fan) / 425F / gas 7.

6. Brush the baguettes with beaten egg and sprinkle with sesame seeds, then slash across the tops with a knife.

7. Transfer the tray to the top shelf of the oven then quickly throw a small cupful of water onto the oven floor and close the door.

8. Bake for 25-30 minutes or until the loaves sound hollow when you tap them underneath.

White cob loaf

MAKES: 2 | PREP TIME: 3 HOURS | COOKING TIME: 35-40 MINUTES

INGREDIENTS

400 g / 14 oz / 2 ⅔ cups strong white bread flour,
plus extra for dusting

½ tsp easy-blend dried yeast

1 tbsp caster (superfine) sugar

1 tsp fine sea salt

1 tbsp olive oil

METHOD

1. Mix together the flour, yeast, sugar and salt.
   Stir the oil into 280ml of warm water then
   stir it into the dry ingredients.

2. Knead the mixture on a lightly oiled surface
   with your hands for 10 minutes or until
   smooth and elastic.

3. Leave the dough to rest in a lightly
   oiled bowl, covered with oiled cling film,
   for 1–2 hours or until doubled in size.

4. Knead it for 2 more minutes then split it into
   2 even pieces and shape into 2 round loaves.

5. Transfer the cobs to a greased baking tray
   and cover with oiled cling film. Leave to
   prove for 1 hour or until doubled in size.

6. Meanwhile, preheat the oven to 220°C
   (200°C fan) / 425F / gas 7.

7. Dust the cobs with flour and slash a cross in
   the tops with a knife.

8. Transfer the tray to the top shelf of the oven
   then quickly throw a small cupful of water
   onto the oven floor and close the door.

9. Bake for 35-40 minutes or until the loaves
   sound hollow when you tap them
   underneath.

10. Transfer to a wire rack and leave to cool.

Cheese and herb loaf

SERVES: 8 | PREP TIME: 20 MINUTES | COOKING TIME: 55 MINUTES

INGREDIENTS

300 g / 10 ½ oz / 2 cups self-raising flour

2 tsp baking powder

250 g / 9 oz / 1 ¼ cups butter, softened

5 large eggs

100 g / 3 ½ oz / 1 cup Cheddar, grated

2 tbsp flat leaf parsley, chopped

2 tbsp chives, chopped

METHOD

1. Preheat the oven to 170°C (150°C fan) / 340F / gas 3 and line a large loaf tin with non-stick baking paper.

2. Sieve the flour and baking powder into a mixing bowl and add the butter and eggs.

3. Beat the mixture with an electric whisk for 4 minutes or until smooth and well whipped.

4. Fold in the cheese and herbs, then scrape the mixture into the loaf tin.

5. Bake for 55 minutes or until a skewer inserted in the centre comes out clean.

6. Transfer the cake to a wire rack and leave to cool completely before serving.

Spelt bread

MAKES: 1 | PREP TIME: 3 HOURS | COOKING TIME: 35-40 MINUTES

INGREDIENTS

200 g / 7 oz / 1 ⅓ cups strong white bread flour, plus extra for dusting

200 g / 7 oz / 1 ⅓ cups spelt flour

½ tsp easy-blend dried yeast

1 tbsp caster (superfine) sugar

1 tsp fine sea salt

1 tbsp olive oil

METHOD

1. Mix together the flours, yeast, sugar and salt. Stir in the oil and 280ml of warm water.

2. Knead on a lightly oiled surface for 10 minutes or until the dough is elastic.

3. Leave the dough to rest, covered with oiled cling film, for 1–2 hours or until doubled in size.

4. Knead the dough for 2 more minutes, then shape it into a round loaf.

5. Transfer the loaf to a greased baking tray and cover again with oiled cling film. Leave to prove for 1 hour or until doubled in size.

6. Preheat the oven to 220°C (200°C fan) / 430F / gas 7.

7. When the dough has risen, score the top with a knife and dust with flour.

8. Bake for 35-40 minutes. Transfer the bread to a wire rack and leave to cool.

Onion bread

MAKES: 1 | PREP TIME: 3 HOURS | COOKING TIME: 50-55 MINUTES

INGREDIENTS

2 large onions, peeled, quartered and sliced

3 tbsp olive oil

300 g / 10 ½ oz / 2 cups strong white bread flour,
plus extra for dusting

100 g / 3 ½ oz / ⅔ cup stoneground wholemeal flour

½ tsp easy-blend dried yeast

1 tbsp caster (superfine) sugar

1 tsp fine sea salt

2 tbsp black onion seeds

METHOD

1. Gently fry the onions in the oil for 15 minutes or until starting to caramelise. Leave to cool.

2. Mix together the flours, yeast, sugar and salt. Stir the onions and onion seeds into 280ml of warm water and stir into the dry ingredients.

3. Knead the mixture on a lightly oiled surface for 10 minutes or until the dough is smooth and elastic.

4. Leave the dough to rest in a lightly oiled bowl, covered with oiled cling film, for 1–2 hours.

5. Roll the dough into a fat sausage. Turn it 90° and roll it tightly the other way then tuck the ends under and transfer the dough to a lined loaf tin, keeping the seam underneath.

6. Cover the tin with oiled cling film and leave for 1 hour.

7. Preheat the oven to 220°C (200°C fan) / 425F / gas 7.

8. Bake the loaf for 35–40 minutes or until the underneath sounds hollow when tapped.

Parmesan rolls

MAKES: 12 | PREP TIME: 3 HOURS | COOKING TIME: 15-20 MINUTES

INGREDIENTS

400 g / 14 oz / 2 ⅔ cups strong white bread flour

½ tsp easy-blend dried yeast

1 tbsp caster (superfine) sugar

1 tsp fine sea salt

1 tbsp olive oil

100 g / 3 ½ oz / 1 cup Parmesan, finely grated

METHOD

1. In a large bowl, mix together the flour, yeast, sugar and salt. Stir in the oil, Parmesan and 280ml of warm water.

2. Knead the mixture on a lightly oiled surface with your hands for 10 minutes or until smooth and elastic.

3. Leave the dough to rest in a lightly oiled bowl, covered with oiled cling film, for 1–2 hours.

4. Knead it for 2 more minutes then split it into 12 even pieces and shape into rolls.

5. Transfer the rolls to a greased baking tray and cover with oiled cling film. Leave to prove for 1 hour.

6. Preheat the oven to 220°C (200°C fan) / 425F/ gas 7.

7. Cut a cross in the top of each roll and transfer the tray to the top shelf of the oven.

8. Bake for 15–20 minutes or until the rolls sound hollow when you tap them underneath.

9. Transfer to a wire rack and leave to cool.

Sesame and poppy seed focaccia

MAKES: 6 | PREP TIME: 3 HOURS | COOKING TIME: 25-35 MINUTES

INGREDIENTS

300 g / 10 ½ oz / 2 cups strong white bread flour

½ tsp easy-blend dried yeast

1 tsp fine sea salt

2 tbsp olive oil

TO FINISH:

50 ml / 1 ¾ fl. oz / ¼ cup olive oil

50 ml / 1 ¾ fl. oz / ¼ cup warm water

½ tsp fine sea salt

1 tbsp sesame seeds

1 tbsp poppy seeds

METHOD

1. Mix together the flour, yeast and salt. Stir in the oil and 280ml of warm water.

2. Knead the mixture on a lightly oiled surface for 10 minutes or until smooth and elastic.

3. Leave the dough to rest, covered with oiled cling film, for 1-2 hours or until doubled in size.

4. Oil a rectangular cake tin then stretch out the dough to cover the base.

5. Cover the focaccia with oiled cling film and leave to prove for 1 hour or until doubled in size.

6. Preheat the oven to 220°C (200°C fan) / 425F / gas 7.

7. Put the oil, water and salt in a jar and shake well. Pour it all over the dough then sprinkle with the seeds.

8. Bake for 25-35 minutes or until the top is golden and the base is cooked through.

9. Leave to cool on a wire rack before cutting into squares.

Crusty farmhouse rolls

MAKES: 12 | PREP TIME: 3 HOURS 20 MINUTES | COOKING TIME: 15-20 MINUTES

INGREDIENTS

350 g / 12 ½ oz/ 2 ⅓ cups strong white bread flour, plus extra for dusting

50 g / 1 ¾ oz / ⅓ cup stoneground wholemeal flour

½ tsp easy-blend dried yeast

1 tbsp caster (superfine) sugar

1 tsp fine sea salt

1 tbsp olive oil

METHOD

1. Mix together the flours, yeast, sugar and salt. Stir in the oil and 280ml of warm water. Knead the mixture on a lightly oiled surface with your hands for 10 minutes.

2. Leave the dough to rest in an oiled bowl covered with cling film, for 2 hours. Knead again then split into 12 even pieces. Shape into rolls.

3. Transfer the rolls to a greased baking tray. Cover with oiled cling film. Leave to prove for 1 hour.

4. Meanwhile, preheat the oven to 220°C (200°C fan) / 425F / gas 7.

5. Dust the rolls with flour. Slash the tops with a knife. Transfer the tray to the top shelf of the oven then throw a small cupful of water onto the oven floor and close the door.

6. Bake for 15-20 minutes or until the rolls sound hollow when you tap them underneath. Transfer to a wire rack and leave to cool.

Sun-dried tomato bread

MAKES: 1 | PREP TIME: 2 HOURS 30 MINUTES | COOKING TIME: 35-40 MINUTES

INGREDIENTS

200 g / 7 oz / 1 ⅓ cups strong white bread flour,
plus extra for dusting

200 g / 7 oz / 1 ⅓ cups stoneground wholemeal flour

½ tsp easy-blend dried yeast

1 tbsp caster (superfine) sugar

1 tsp fine sea salt

150 g / 5 ½ oz / ¾ cup sun-dried tomatoes
in oil, drained

1 tbsp olive oil

METHOD

1. Mix the flours, yeast, sugar, salt and tomatoes.
   Stir in the oil and 280ml warm water. Knead the
   mixture on an oiled surface for 10 minutes, then
   leave the dough to rest in an oiled bowl for 1 hour.

2. Roll the dough with your hands into a fat sausage,
   then turn it 90° and roll it tightly the other way.
   Tuck the ends under and transfer the dough to the
   tin, keeping the seam underneath.

3. Cover the tin loosely with oiled cling film and
   leave to prove somewhere warm for 45 minutes.

4. Preheat the oven to 220°C (200°C fan) / 425F / gas 7.

5. Transfer the tin to the top shelf of the oven.
   Throw a cupful of water onto the floor of the oven
   and close the door.

6. Bake for 35-40 minutes or until the loaf sounds
   hollow when you tap it underneath.

Tuscan saltless bread

MAKES: 1 | PREP TIME: 3 HOURS | COOKING TIME: 35-40 MINUTES

INGREDIENTS

400 g / 14 oz / 2 ⅔ cups strong white bread flour,
plus extra for dusting

½ tsp easy-blend dried yeast

2 tbsp olive oil

300 ml / 10 ½ fl. oz / 1 ⅓ cup warm water

METHOD

1. Mix together the flour and yeast. Stir the oil into 280ml of warm water, then stir it into the dry ingredients.

2. Knead the mixture on a lightly oiled surface with your hands for 10 minutes or until smooth and elastic.

3. Leave the dough to rest in a lightly oiled bowl, covered with oiled cling film, for 1–2 hours or until doubled in size.

4. Knead it for 2 more minutes, then shape into a round loaf.

5. Transfer the loaf to a greased baking tray and cover with oiled cling film. Leave to prove for 1 hour or until doubled in size.

6. Meanwhile, preheat the oven to 220°C (200°C fan) / 425F / gas 7.

7. Dust the loaf with flour and slash the top with a knife.

8. Transfer the tray to the top shelf of the oven then quickly throw a small cupful of water onto the oven floor and close the door.

9. Bake for 35–40 minutes or until the loaf sounds hollow when you tap it underneath.

10. Transfer to a wire rack and leave to cool.

Wholemeal cob loaf

MAKES: 2 | PREP TIME: 3 HOURS | COOKING TIME: 35-40 MINUTES

INGREDIENTS

300 g / 10 ½ oz / 2 cups stoneground
wholemeal flour

100 g / 3 ½ oz / ½ cup strong white bread flour,
plus extra for dusting

½ tsp easy-blend dried yeast

2 tbsp caster (superfine) sugar

1 tsp fine sea salt

1 tbsp olive oil

METHOD

1. Mix together the flours, yeast, sugar and salt.
   Stir the oil and 280ml of warm water into the
   dry ingredients. Knead the mixture on an
   oiled surface for 10 minutes.

2. Leave the dough to rest in a lightly oiled bowl,
   covered with oiled cling film, for 1–2 hours.

3. Knead it for 2 more minutes then split it into
   2 even pieces and shape into 2 round loaves.
   Transfer the cobs to a greased baking tray
   and cover with oiled cling film. Leave to
   prove for 1 hour.

4. Meanwhile, preheat the oven to 220°C
   (200°C fan) / 425F / gas 7.

5. Dust with flour and slash across the tops
   with a knife.

6. Transfer the tray to the oven then quickly
   throw a small cupful of water onto the oven
   floor and close the door.

7. Bake for 35–40 minutes or until the loaves
   sound hollow when you tap the underneath.

217

Garlic mushroom bread

MAKES: 1 | PREP TIME: 2 HOURS 30 MINUTES | COOKING TIME: 35-40 MINUTES

INGREDIENTS

200 g / 7 oz / 1 ⅓ cups strong white bread flour

200 g / 7 oz / 1 ⅓ cups rye flour

1 tsp easy-blend dried yeast

1 tbsp caster (superfine) sugar

1 tsp fine sea salt

1 tbsp olive oil

FOR THE MUSHROOMS:

50 g / 1 ¾ oz / ¼ cup butter

300 g / 10 ½ oz chestnut mushrooms, sliced

2 cloves of garlic, crushed

50 g / 1 ¾ oz flat-leaved parsley, chopped

METHOD

1. Mix together the flours, yeast, sugar and salt. Stir the oil into 280ml of warm water and mix with the dry ingredients.

2. Knead the dough on a lightly oiled surface for 10 minutes or until smooth and elastic.

3. Leave the dough to rest, covered with oiled cling film, for 1-2 hours.

4. Melt the butter in a sauté pan and add the mushrooms and plenty of salt and pepper. Cook for 10 minutes. Add the garlic and parsley and cook for 2 minutes. Leave to cool.

5. Knead the mushrooms into the dough and shape into a square loaf.

6. Transfer it to a greased baking tray, cover with oiled cling film and prove until doubled in size.

7. Preheat the oven to 220°C (200°C fan) / 425F / gas 7.

8. Transfer the tray to the top shelf of the oven, then quickly throw a small cupful of water onto the floor of the oven and close the door.

9. Bake for 35-40 minutes or until the loaf sounds hollow when tapped underneath. Transfer to a wire rack and leave to cool.

Parmesan olive shortbreads

MAKES: 16 | PREP TIME: 20 MINUTES | COOKING TIME: 15-20 MINUTES

INGREDIENTS

150 g / 5 oz / ⅔ cup butter, cubed

230 g / 8 oz / 1 ½ cup plain (all-purpose) flour

50 g / 1 ¾ oz / ½ cup Parmesan, grated

50 g / 1 ¾ oz / ⅓ cup black olives, pitted
and finely chopped

sea salt flakes for sprinkling

METHOD

1. Preheat the oven to 180°C (160°C fan) / 350F /
   gas 4 and line a baking tray with
   greaseproof paper.

2. Rub the butter into the flour and stir in the
   Parmesan and olives.

3. Knead until the mixture forms a smooth
   dough. Form into a cylinder 6 cm in diameter.

4. Slice the roll into 1 cm thick slices and spread
   them out on the baking tray.

5. Bake the biscuits for 15-20 minutes, turning the
   tray round halfway through.

6. Sprinkle the biscuits with sea salt flakes then
   transfer to a wire rack and leave to cool.

Cheese wafer biscuits

MAKES: 36 | PREP TIME: 10 MINUTES | COOKING TIME: 8-10 MINUTES

INGREDIENTS

225 g / 8 oz / 1 cup butter

½ tsp cayenne pepper

175 g / 6 oz / 1 ¾ cups Red Leicester cheese, grated

300 g / 10 ½ oz / 2 cups plain (all-purpose) flour

METHOD

1. Preheat the oven to 180°C (160°C fan) / 350F / gas 4 and line 2 baking sheets with greaseproof paper.

2. Melt the butter with the cayenne pepper in a saucepan.

3. Stir in the cheese and flour, beating rapidly to form a paste.

4. Use a teaspoon to portion the mixture onto the baking trays and spread the biscuits out thinly with the back of the spoon.

5. Bake in batches for 8–10 minutes.

6. Leave the biscuits to harden on the tray for a few minutes then transfer them to a wire rack to cool.

INDEX